MAPPING
CHRISTIAN
EDUCATION

MAPPING CHRISTIAN EDUCATION

Approaches to Congregational Learning

EDITOR

JACK L. SEYMOUR

ABINGDON PRESS
Nashville

MAPPING CHRISTIAN EDUCATION
APPROACHES TO CONGREGATIONAL LEARNING

Copyright © 1997 by Abingdon Press

All rights reserved.

This book is printed on recycled, acid-free paper.

Library of Congress Cataloging-in-Publication Data

Seymour, Jack L. (Jack Lee), 1948–
    Mapping Christian education : approaches to congregational
learning / editor, Jack L. Seymour.
        p.   cm.
    Includes bibliographical references.
    ISBN 0-687-00812-3 (pbk. : alk. paper)
    1. Christian education—Philosophy.
BV1464.M36   1997
268—dc21   96-51888
                                                                                              CIP

Scripture quotations, unless otherwise indicated, are from the New Revised Standard Version Bible, copyright © 1989, by the Division of Christian Education of the National Council of the Churches of Christ in the United States of America.

Scripture quotations noted KJV are from the King James Version of the Bible.

Material from the February 1996 and March 1996 issues of *P.A.C.E.* is used by permission.

Material from the spring 1997 issue of *Religious Education* is used by permission.

99 00 01 02 03 04 05 06—10 9 8 7 6 5 4 3

MANUFACTURED IN THE UNITED STATES OF AMERICA

CONTENTS

ACKNOWLEDGMENTS

"There is no one clue, no dominant theory." With these words, educator Sara Little acknowledges today's pluralism in the field of Christian education. A "growing group of scholars" is "producing a spectrum of theories and divergent interests."[1] This vitality is itself a sign of hope. Educators are seeking to address the cries of the culture, the integrity of theological traditions, and the experiences of people.

Little further argues, "Education is recognized as a field requiring interdisciplinary collaboration. It is public. It is diverse. It is dependent on a living religion for vitality."[2] How a living religion contributes a future to persons, human communities, and the created world is the passion motivating Christian educators. Interdisciplinary and public dialogue is needed about the future, about religious experience, about partnerships among religious traditions, and ultimately about God's dream for a whole and just creation.

I thank those who have participated in collaboration to create *Mapping Christian Education:* Elizabeth Caldwell, Margaret Ann Crain, Maria Harris, Donald Miller, Gabriel Moran, Robert O'Gorman, and Daniel Schipani. Their work reveals clues to Christian education and meanings of faith for today. I also thank those who collaborated fifteen years ago in *Contemporary Approaches to Christian Education:* Charles Foster, Sara Little, Donald Miller, Allen Moore, and Carol Wehrheim, as well as Young Taek Lim and Kazuhiro Okuda who have translated that book into Korean and Japanese respectively. They are partners in a living religion.

I thank my colleagues in Christian education in the Chicago Cluster of Theological Schools who encourage one another through rich public dialogue. At Garrett-Evangelical Theological Seminary, I thank the administration who have supported this project with a research grant and my colleague, Linda Vogel, who creates safe and hospitable spaces for learning and interdisciplinary conversation.

I especially thank my research colleague, Margaret Ann Crain, for her encouragement throughout the process of this book. Her assistance with editing has helped make its visions clearer. As we have listened to people of God question, speak of religious experiences, and express their searches for faith and vocation, we have engaged the divergent interests and passions of a "living" religion.

Indeed, education is an interdisciplinary collaboration. It is public and it is diverse. I invite you to join in this collaboration. As we live our religion, may we listen to the people of God express meanings for their lives, may we seek to renew the traditions of faith, and, above all, may we live God's vision of wholeness and justice.

Jack L. Seymour
Epiphany 1996

1

Approaches to Christian Education

JACK L. SEYMOUR

A retired human resources director for a large public utility and a longtime Sunday school teacher, Frank Donnell, talked about the church and its educational ministry. "But this is one of the challenges," he noted. "Somehow we have not made it possible or easy for people to be theological in their everyday relationships and conversations. . . . When we talk about faith, it sounds artificial or forced. . . . And, yet, it's the dominant element in so many of our lives." He wondered, "Why aren't we able to communicate faith?"[1] He was concerned about why it seems so difficult to talk about faith and to connect it with daily living.

Thinking about his Sunday school class, he spoke of his desire to help people expand their ideas and clarify how the resources of the Bible and the Christian faith assist them in their everyday lives. People need help in making life decisions. As his class has aged, as people have retired and lost spouses, and as health has declined, he has seen fear in these people's eyes and puzzlement about the meaning of life and about their continuing vocations as Christians in the world.

He too knows the joy and pain of living. His father died when he was young, a brother died much too early of diabetes, and a son-in-law died in an automobile accident. Presently, Frank and his daughter care for his wife, who, because of Alzheimer's disease, is confined to a bed in the living room of their home.

Frank is always learning: For instance, when he was in his early sixties and nearing retirement, he attended an intense human relations workshop, and he has always read widely on a variety of topics. He decided to retire because he believed his company was shifting its focus from service to profit. Frank Donnell knows the struggles of connecting life to faith. Teaching Sunday school is a joy. He considers the texts of the faith and wonders about living.

9

"Why aren't we able to communicate faith?" Why do we have so much difficulty being "theological" in "everyday relationships and conversations"? He traces this difficulty to education. "We ought to teach that there is a process to learning. . . . If we could teach it, it might help people in their religious growth." Christian education needs to be a process that helps people face life.

He participated in focused conversations with three other parishioners in his church, talking about their faith stories and their experiences of God and the church. They shared theological convictions that guided their everyday living. They also talked about the questions that trouble them and their search for meaning for their lives. Frank commented on the conversations, "What struck me is how much searching there is, and—interestingly—not too many discoveries. . . . We're all searching and everybody's sure that there's something valuable out there." They were being theological in their everyday relationships. They were talking about faith as a dominant reality in their lives. Yet, Frank was puzzled about the lack of "discoveries, insights, or revelations" the group could claim. He asked if we did not recognize the revelations that were present, were there none, or did we just settle for old patterns and not see God's new action in our midst?

Frank raises profoundly the question of how we educate for faith, how we make it possible "to be theological" in our everyday relationships. How do we connect the experiences of life and the meanings of the faith tradition? How do we consider the wealth of information and values at our disposal? How do we discern how to live as Christians in a world of rapid change, increasing diversity, ethnic violence, enhanced networks of communication, limited resources, improved technologies of health, and mounting gaps of wealth and opportunity?[2] How do we recognize God's revelations and how do we transcend old patterns to respond to what God is doing new in our midst?

A small group in another congregation spoke about struggling to integrate faith and life. They called it "thrashing in the night." Thomas Jarrell, a publisher, noted, "There are lots of people exploring. They are attempting to keep the faith . . . trying to translate the meaning of religious experience into languages consistent with the other languages that we deal with everyday."

How does the church and its educational ministry help people "translate" faith into life?

Translating, interpreting, and empowering are tasks for Christian education. The issues that call us to Christian education are the issues of life as we struggle to be faithful. The settings are varied, and can be any place we learn about the faith and connect it to our living. Through the church's ministries of worship, care, mission, and community, we reflect with others on the meanings of our lives and our faithfulness. Christian education provides a context in which people engage life with the great traditions of faith, religious experiences, and the resources of our cultures. We seek to know what our lives mean in light of God and how we are called to participate in God's grace, love, and hope in the midst of life.

EDUCATION IN THE CHRISTIAN COMMUNITY

Christian education is as old as Christian faith. Jesus was a rabbi, a teacher, who gathered disciples and preached to crowds about the new life that God was bringing. Building on his Jewish faith, he reminded people of their values and commitments. He pointed to God breaking into history calling people to new meanings and new ways of living. He challenged people to be faithful.

After Jesus' death, disciples followed his example of preaching about new life—new ways of understanding themselves and their world and new ways of living in light of Jesus the Christ. They taught in synagogues, prayed with groups of people, and preached about meanings that had graced them. The stories about Jesus and God's amazing acts were remembered. The sayings of Jesus were memorized. Christian leaders wrote letters answering questions that were raised in the new churches. Instruction sought to resolve conflicts among Christians and provide tools for them to witness about faith in the wider culture.

Eventually, Gospels were written to clarify the meanings of Jesus' life and death. These Gospels provided portraits of Jesus, but more than that they taught people about the meaning of life and the ways of living. Luke, for example, told the people how to be the church, how to be the hands and feet of Jesus until the day of the Kingdom. These traditions of Jesus and the church taught people who they were, what was expected of them, and how they were to act toward each other.

Some of the teaching was formal. Missionaries went from community to community spreading the good news and instructing people in the meanings and actions they were to embody. Other teaching took place in families, as people shared table fellowship, or in the celebration of worship. Most often people learned as they shared life with other Christians. For example, the poor Christians living in tenement houses in Rome learned how to be faithful together through sharing meals, worshiping, talking about life, and providing for each other (Romans 16). People learned the faith as they lived the faith with others.

Early centers of scholarship and teaching were established. Church leaders sought to clarify the meaning of Christian faith in the religiously diverse Roman Empire. Most of the teaching occurred when people confronted conflicts over variant theological positions, learned to live together, and witnessed to their experiences of God.

After the acceptance of Christianity as the official religion of the Roman Empire, teaching occurred even more through the people's daily living. The architecture of churches proclaimed God's presence, the bells of churches told time, plays in the streets reminded people of the major meanings of life and faith, and the rules of daily life were significantly influenced by church leaders. While there were many settings for formal instruction, most people learned the faith as they practiced it. Life and faith were integrated.

While life and faith are not integrated in modern U.S. society, most people have learned the faith, reflected on its meanings for their lives, and discovered ways of living by participating in Christian communities. For example, by the middle of the 1800s, Roman Catholic families in the United States found that daily life emphasized the Protestant experience. Most public schools taught Protestant beliefs and used texts that referred to Protestantism as normative. In response, Roman Catholics created communities where church, parochial school, and daily life were intimately

12

related. Roman Catholic children learned the faith by attending church schools, living in the vicinity of other Catholics, worshiping together, and experiencing common values taught by parents who themselves were influenced by parish life.

Other religious groups also knew the power of learning by participating. The Amish, for example, set their communities apart from the wider society and its defined patterns of living together. People learned faith by intimately participating in day-to-day decisions. They learned what it meant to be Amish and how Amish people behaved.

Even today much of our learning takes place as we participate in families and communities. Yet, schools and classrooms carry the responsibility of directly teaching the values and tools needed to live in society. Professional schools teach the skills necessary for service to the wider community. Language schools teach immigrants to communicate in a new culture.

Religious education too has become centered in schools. In the 1800s Sunday schools flourished in the U.S., catechetical instruction was formalized and taught in churches and parochial schools, and many local churches and denominations founded schools and colleges to teach young people the skills of life in a faith context. By the late 1800s, official courses in Christian religious education were taught in colleges and seminaries. Denominations provided teacher training programs in instructional methods at campground gatherings, like Chautauqua, New York. Religious orders taught nuns and brothers how to teach in church-sponsored schools.

The academic discipline of religious education was recognized in the first decade of the twentieth century at nearly the same time the Religious Education Association was founded in 1903 in Chicago to link the best in religion and education. Throughout the twentieth century, this discipline has been comprehensive in its approaches to Christian education. Of course, schools and classes dominated the thinking as churches both copied and influenced the forms of education in the wider society. Yet, worship was understood to be educational. Through preaching and liturgy, people participated in the meanings of the faith and connected them to living. Moreover, the power of the church to educate was recognized. Early Christian educators talked about the church as a "school of Christian living" and sought to coordinate its school with fellowship and training efforts such as scouts, youth groups, men's groups, and women's missionary societies; with worship and preaching; and with the church's ministries to the community. While the language was often that of instruction—teaching the Bible or doctrine—and the concern was often with personal growth, approaches to education were advocated that enhanced schooling, examined the parish as a learning community, and sent people into mission.

CONTEMPORARY APPROACHES TO CHRISTIAN EDUCATION

Our convictions about education affect the way we structure congregational life. For example, with a focus on action and mission, educational leaders organize projects where people minister. By engaging life problems, people reflect on what they have learned about faith, others, themselves, life, and ministry. With a focus on faith community, educators attend to learning by participating. They are concerned with how church and community powerfully teach values and ways of living. With a focus on instruction, leaders are concerned about teachers and the content (curriculum) that they teach. They also attend to how this content is mastered and how persons connect it to living. With a focus on the person, people are helped to integrate the faith within their own life stories and continue to grow in faith.

In 1982, Donald Miller and I edited *Contemporary Approaches to Christian Education* to clarify a variety of themes that were directing church education.[3] The 1970s had been a time of renewal in the field. Multiple voices explored the relationship of education and culture, the research on human development, and numerous strategies of teaching.[4] *Contemporary Approaches* helped bring some order to those rapid developments.

Contemporary Approaches described what was happening in Christian education. The congregation as a setting for education and the relationship of education to mission were discussed. The possibilities and limitations of schooling were examined. Methods of teaching were considered that included both cognitive and affective components. The role of theological methods to renew the tradition was explored. And the contribution of psychological research to church education was considered.

In the midst of the vitality of new voices, five primary themes emerged: (1) religious instruction, (2) faith community, (3) development, (4) liberation, and (5) interpretation. We saw these as alternate filters shaping the field. Instruction emphasized the structures of formal education and ordered learning within the church. The faith community captured the power of the life of the congregation to teach. Development built upon psychological research about individual growth. Liberation grew out of the efforts of Latin American liberation theologies to empower people to live the reign of God in the midst of oppression. And interpretation focused on the ways education connected faith and everyday life. This "map" of the field provided a way to track and explore some of the developments.

Today the paradigm of Christian education that relies on the practices of public education is under considerable scrutiny. Contemporary studies look to congregational life and public mission for Christian education theory. Therefore, in the last decade, even more attention has been given to the relationship of biblical methodologies, the study of religions, and the theology to Christian education. In addition, the patterns of learning embedded in ethnic experiences have received increased attention. The relationship of human development psychology and Christian education is evaluated through gender and ethnic lenses. Furthermore, Christian education has focused on empowering laity to embody discipleship in the world.

MAPPING CHRISTIAN EDUCATION

Where is the field today? What concerns empower the dialogue? In our culture, we are in an era of fear and anxiety. In fact, many believe that as a culture we have lost our way. A recent Gallup poll shows that while 87 percent of the U.S. population believes that religion is important, 67 percent believes that its influence is declining.[5] The old mainline churches are now called the sideline. Law professor Stephen Carter, writes that our culture is *The Culture of Disbelief* in which God is pushed from public discourse to the private parts of our lives.[6] We are puzzled about how religion will address the future.

The widening gap of rich and poor, the explosion of ethnic conflict and terrorism, the resurgence of authoritarian religions, the struggle over public priorities, and the growing nihilism of many urban youth who see no future are distressing. In the conversations in which Frank Donnell and Thomas Jarrell participated (described at the beginning of this chapter), these fears are reflected. An environmental engineer, Cynthia Dayton, noted that she "wrestles" with God to understand and respond to suffering. Charles Eldridge added, "It hurts me to see the violence in the world today and the way that young people feel about the future of the world." Personal suffering and the brokenness of the world are two of the issues that draw us into reflection on our responsibilities as Christians.

How can the church be engaged during this time of limits and possibilities? The church is called to be open to the world, open to diversity, and proclaim a faith that addresses personal needs and connects us with public life. In a world "in agony," where fear aches at the edges, where the human project is threatened, and where ways of truth change, religion is a key resource to confront the future with grace and hope.[7]

Theologian Douglas John Hall argues that we have three options of responding to the terror about the future.[8] One is *denial*: We close our eyes to the future and spend our psychic energies holding down our fears. A second option is *despair*: We give up and believe that the future is unredeemable. We try to anesthetize ourselves to the pain. The result of these two options is ultimately self-defeating. The third option is *hope* that empowers action. Yet, hope cannot be grounded on empty promises or the denial of pain. Hope is only possible if we face pain directly. Theologically, hope is grounded in the Cross, that image of confusion and pain that includes disciples crying and acknowledging their loss. The Cross is, at the same time, a powerful image of hope and resurrection.

Here is the context for Christian education: In a world of fear and anxiety, we must find ways of acknowledging the lives of people. We must confront issues together by joining into the fray of history as a time full of possibility. The church must enter into the terror with the proclamation that the God of history knows the pain and suffers with us. As Psalm 130:1 proclaims, "Out of the depths I cry to you, O LORD." Hope is in the recognition of both brokenness and possibilities for transformation. We learn to be faithful by reflecting on the brokenness and possibilities in the experiences of our lives, and the social contexts in which they emerge in communities of care and mission that are seeking to be a part of a hope-filled, grace-filled, and inclusive future. Interpretation and empowerment are central to all approaches of Christian education.

In his comprehensive study of faith, historian of world religions Wilfred Cantwell Smith argues that one learns a religion as if one were in a dance. "One does not 'have' a dance; one takes part in it. The pattern one may learn from others; but a dance pattern does not become a dance until someone dances it."[9] A religion is learned by participating in its living vitality. Religion is never the same for every worshiper. Religion becomes real as each person lives and responds in community.

For Smith, living life religiously is a "complex interaction" of (1) "an accumulating religious *tradition*" that one has in part inherited, (2) "the particular *personality*" that each person brings, (3) "the particular *environment*" in which each happens to live, "new every morning," and (4) "the *transcendent* reality" to which the tradition points and in relation to which one lives. A religion is learned when one comes to know the heritage of those who went before and the meanings that inspired them. Yet, religion takes on a unique character because of the contexts and the communities in which we participate, and the personalities that we have. Speaking of a Muslim group, Smith says: "Theirs was no academic or purely theoretical quest, but a serious wrestling with the issue of what is God's will in the novel, perplexing, ever-changing world of our twentieth century. What does it mean, they were concerned to know, to be Muslim in the challenging vicissitudes of modern life and thought?"[10]

That too is true of Christian faith. We are engaged in a serious wrestling with a perplexing and ever-changing world asking how can we be faithful in the challenging vicissitudes of life, how can we contribute to the healing and justice of God in the midst of life? Education in faith is rooted in knowing a tradition, interacting with a community of meaning and memory, responding out of an individual personality, and moving into the world. Instruction in tradition, living in a community of faith, exploring one's self, and facing the world are the key elements of learning a faith tradition, interpreting its meanings in life, and being empowered to engage the world.

Christian education is a conversation for living, a seeking to use the resources of the faith and cultural traditions to move into an open future of justice and hope. We need to partner with people who are seeking to be faithful for a history full of anguish and possibility. As Frank Donnell asked, How do we make it possible "for people to be theological in their everyday relationships and conversations?" As Thomas Jarrell questioned, How do we help people "translate" faith language with everyday language? As Cynthia Dayton and Charles Eldridge wondered, How do we respond to the cries of suffering and the pain of brokenness? How does the church help us to be honest about and engage our everyday relationships?

That we seek to answer these questions demonstrates the vitality in Christian education today. Some contemporary theories focus on the congregation, others on the church's mission to the public, on culturally diverse and multicultural patterns of education, on theological reflection, on human development and spirituality, and on the role of religious schools in teaching faith content. Helping people interpret the faith and be empowered for living inspires the search for approaches to Christian education.

APPROACHES TO CHRISTIAN EDUCATION

In the chapters that follow, four of these themes are highlighted as they provide directions for the field of Christian education:

(1) the mission of the church in the world, (2) the role of the faith community, (3) the understanding of the person, and (4) the place of instruction. Many of the concerns in these essays overlap. However, each is a powerful portrayal of ways to shape Christian education. Each is written by a scholar who has made a significant contribution to education, the church, and ministry. By reviewing each writer's portraits of education, we may be more clearly aware of the themes that influence our conversations and the ways we can embody education in the church and culture.

Transformation—Daniel Schipani explores social transformation as a frame of reference for Christian education. Transformation becomes both the goal and process of education until God's kingdom of justice and love is fully embodied. Congregations teach as they engage people and communities to promote faithful citizenship and social transformation.

People learn what it means to be faithful Christians, partnering with God, when they participate in the compassionate church reaching into the world with ministries of care, justice, and transformation. We learn as we see our world through social and theological analysis, as we judge our actions in light of the faith tradition and social analysis, and as we engage in faithful action. Learning is rooted in action as we plan for it, engage in it, and reflect on it. Questions of God's mission direct our thinking about Christian education. We learn and are transformed as we participate in transforming ministries.

Faith Community—Robert O'Gorman defines community as the content and process of Christian education. Learning the faith occurs as we participate in a faith community that seeks to promote authentic human development, that is, which enhances the relationship of persons to others, communities, and the cosmos.

Grounded in the loneliness of modern life, small groups have emerged as a means of assisting persons to meet needs, find support, and move into the world. Yet, small groups can become insulating and further fragment our common life. The same is true of faith communities. Our identities are clearly and profoundly reinforced in faith communities where we learn ways of living and responding. Yet, if the faith community does not launch us into a concern for the emerging community of all creation, it too is fragmenting.

Communities of faith need to push us through the intimate group of care into the larger world connecting people, communities, and the cosmos, as well as into relationships and communion. Through the dynamics of service, reflection, and action, we come to know the story of the faith, to connect our individual stories, and to engage in appropriate ways of living. Community is in genesis. How we participate in this genesis is the central question of education.

Spiritual Development—Maria Harris and Gabriel Moran examine the personal dimension of learning. The faith is ultimately embodied in each person and, in turn, persons work together in communities. While the ultimate goal of spiritual development is calling persons into relationship, friendship, care, and justice with others and the creation, the starting point for education is the person.

Each person possesses capacities for inwardness, yet is outwardly related to others and the world. Christian education focuses on both of these dimensions. The person is formed through silence, listening, sabbath, study, and service. The person is guided to a fuller and richer connection with all of life, carrying the resources of the faith tradition, practicing the presence of God, and engaging in partnership with others in the midst of the world. Through Christian education persons touch their own deepest centers of meaning and value and are connected to other persons and the creation in meaning, care, and justice.

Religious Instruction—How do we learn to face the world as Christians? Elizabeth Caldwell describes a formal process of theological reflection, of teaching and learning, where we come to know, interpret, and incarnate the faith. Teachers and learners together as partners dwell in a place of care, reflection, and meaning where we learn a story and a faith in order to live responsibly and faithfully in the face of the world.

Christian education involves formal instruction in the faith, but instruction is best defined as homemaking. We tend to the tasks of creating a safe and intimate environment where the meanings that are deepest to ourselves can be shared and where we come to know what it means to live in the family named Christian. The control and mastery of schooling are replaced by the tending, building, cleaning, nurturing, caring, and knowing of homemaking.

We move from the world to the home and from the home to the world. Questions pass from one to the other. Homecomings are always glorious as we celebrate being together. Homecomings send us out strengthened and directed into care and service.

Map of Approaches to Christian Education

	TRANSFORMATION	FAITH COMMUNITY	SPIRITUAL GROWTH	RELIGIOUS INSTRUCTION
GOAL	Assisting people and communities to promote faithful citizenship and social transformation	Building communities that promote authentic human development; helping persons enact community	Helping persons enhance the inner life and respond with outward action to others and the cosmos	Enabling learners to be grounded in the biblical faith and make connections between the content of the faith and living
TEACHER	Sponsor who invites learners into partnership for reflection and action	Leaders who facilitate small groups and help congregations structure for parish life and mission	Guide or pilgrim on the journey of inner life and outward response with others	Teacher in partnership with learners building a space and process for learning
LEARNER	Free and responsible historical agents	People and communities of faith	Person on a journey	Responsible contributors to a learning process; partners
PROCESS OF EDUCATION	Seeing— Judging— Acting	Service— Reflection— Action	Silence, listening, sabbath, study, service	Theological reflection occurring in knowing, interpreting, living, and doing the faith
CONTEXT	The compassionate church and its ministries in and with the world	The congregation set within a wider community	Any setting where a person engages spiritual formation and social outreach	Homemaking— a learning community that empowers faithful learning across the ages
IMPLICATIONS FOR MINISTRY	Supporting the church's call to become an alternative way of seeing life, of being, and of living	Assisting groups and churches to enact community and reach out into the world	Connecting persons to the deepest resources of life calling them to relationship, friendship, care, and justice	Preparing people with a story and faith to live responsibly and faithfully in the face of the world

EDUCATION FOR PUBLIC LIFE AND MINISTRY

How do we make it possible for people to be theological in their everyday lives? How do we help people translate and connect the language of religious faith with the languages spoken in our daily lives? How do we come to know God's revelations for new life and meaning in the midst of our world? How are we empowered for ministry? Christian education incorporates all of the ways we reflect on, engage in, converse with, and seek to live the faith in the midst of our daily lives. Our meanings, our identities and vocations are always the result of connecting with others, the transcendent reality we experience, and the heritage that forms us in the midst of a historical moment and circumstance.

Moreover, the witness of Christian faith is that God is living in the midst of history, that God is working as partner to create justice, love, and community. Christian education is grounded in history and set loose in the world to enact God's realm of hope and love. Faith matters. Life will be changed by God's leading and our faithful action. Decisions about the content of education, its form and settings, the processes that we use, and our interactions are critical. They define how we seek to know our call and interconnection with all of life. Through Christian education we face the world, explore the deepest meanings of our lives, engage one another, and partner with a God seeking wholeness and meaning for all life.

2

Educating for
Social Transformation

DANIEL S. SCHIPANI

Blessed are the poor in spirit, for theirs is the kingdom of heaven.
Blessed are those who mourn, for they will be comforted.
Blessed are the meek, for they will inherit the earth.
Blessed are those who hunger and thirst for righteousness, for they
   will be filled.
Blessed are the merciful, for they will receive mercy.
Blessed are the pure in heart, for they will see God.
Blessed are the peacemakers, for they will be called children of God.
Blessed are those who are persecuted for righteousness' sake . . .

(Matt. 5:3-10)[1]

A CHURCH'S JOURNEY TOWARD RACIAL JUSTICE
AND RECONCILIATION

Reba Place Church is a congregation of about three hundred members located in Evanston, Illinois, and affiliated with the Mennonite Church and the Church of the Brethren.[2] This intentional community was formed by European American Mennonites in the early 1960s and is located in an integrated urban area in order to address the individualism, materialism, and violence of the dominant culture.

The present population surrounding the church is evenly mixed between African Americans and European Americans, with increasing numbers of Latinos and Cambodian immigrants moving into the neighborhood. Typical members of the congregation tend to be middle class and well schooled. However, in the surrounding neighborhood, the economic status, class, and education levels of the residents are mixed.

The early vision of Reba Place nurtured living in a desegregated neighborhood and invited neighbors into fellowship. Thus, a day care center was started, and apartment buildings were purchased to serve the neighborhood. As friendships were cultivated, African American churches began relating to Reba Place for choir and ministry exchanges and neighborhood ministry.

In the summer of 1991, an adult Sunday school class focused on racial reconciliation. About forty people attended. After deep sharing and explicit education, four small congregational groups called "Living Hope Clusters" began to pray for racial justice and reconciliation and to listen to the leading of God's Spirit. A number of specific actions occurred:

- *a racial reconciliation group started meeting weekly to pray, discuss, and share ideas on how racial reconciliation might be furthered;*
- *an African American minister became one of Reba Place's four elders, thus connecting the church to other ministries and beginning a neighborhood association;*
- *a gospel choir was started that not only sings at Reba Place but has been invited to sing at other churches, a nearby university, denominational regional meetings, and park district celebrations;*
- *a group of four (two women and two men, including two African Americans and two European Americans) received training in antiracism education and organizing;*
- *a number of antiracism workshops were offered, starting with the racial reconciliation group and the leadership team;*
- *weekly small groups were encouraged to examine and act on racial justice and reconciliation (for instance, one group engaged in antiracism activities during Lent and a men's group studied the book* Enter the River*);* [3]
- *five African Americans were invited to join the nine-member joint-leadership committee;*
- *worship services were changed, and a pattern of alternating African American services was devised;*
- *preaching often focused on racial reconciliation;*
- *summer Sunday evening worship services in the neighborhood park were led predominantly by African American church members;*

- *the congregation organized to elect one of its African American members to the local park district board;*
- *worship services celebrated the journey toward racial justice and reconciliation and identified remaining challenges.*

These endeavors of reconciliation have significantly reshaped the life and ministry of Reba Place Church. The faith community has become more racially integrated and African American persons are actively involved in positions of decision making and leadership. The very process of making decisions has changed, sometimes challenging traditional patterns.

Friendships have more readily developed across racial lines. Activities and programs have been assessed in terms of racial justice and reconciliation. Christian education curriculum is being reevaluated and youth ministry planning includes dismantling racism as a priority. The lens of racial justice and reconciliation is also applied to evangelism and the making of disciples through growth groups. Church mission and public ministry have also been enhanced through conducting a neighborhood needs survey, buying other buildings for low income co-ops, and starting an afterschool program for elementary school children. Worship has been transformed as it more faithfully reflects the embraced realities of diversity and inclusiveness. The whole process has often entailed dealing with conflict and the tension of blending reconciliation and peacemaking with the pursuit of justice.

A significant amount of ownership at the grassroots level has kept the congregation moving ahead. These current initiatives are interpreted as living out the vision of Reba Place Church. Some leaders have noted that time-honored ways of functioning have given way to innovation and some risk taking without disastrous results. They are expecting new wineskins for the new wine.

The story of Reba Place's ongoing journey toward racial justice and reconciliation illustrates the challenge and the opportunity of congregational education oriented to both personal and social transformation. Churches also need to confront growing poverty, inequality, economic injustice, violence and militarism, neglect of particular groups of people, unjust justice systems, and other structures that discriminate, marginalize, oppress, and alienate. Furthermore, the church must simultaneously face the manifestations of injustice and suffering in its own midst.

Several assumptions inform the content of this chapter. First, the gospel of the reign of God taught by Jesus is transformative leaven in our world. Christian faith must play a role in the transformation of society and culture. Second, the church's educational ministry is indispensable. Third, congregational education must be grounded on a biblical-theological foundation concerned with liberation, justice, and peace.

THE GOAL: HUMAN EMERGENCE IN THE LIGHT OF THE REIGN OF GOD

The overarching purpose of congregational Christian education, oriented by justice, must be consistent with the church's ministry for the sake of the world. Congregational Christian education consists of *sponsoring human emergence in the light of the reign of God.*

"Sponsoring human emergence." The term *sponsoring* connotes Jesus' prevailing style of educating—a way of being and walking with people characterized by compassionate initiative, hospitable inclusiveness, gentle empowerment, and a generous invitation to partnership and community. Sponsoring includes encouraging, enabling, and guiding in contrast to authoritarian, paternalistic, and manipulative ways of practicing education.[4]

We become partners with God's Spirit at work with, and through, us. In other words, we do not effect liberation, justice, authentic growth, and wholeness; but God does, as Paul reminds us in I Cor. 3:5-11. Nevertheless, God invites us to participate in the fashioning of a new creation as sponsors of human emergence.

Human emergence denotes a process of becoming "more human" in terms of God's gift and promise of freedom and wholeness, living according to the ethical, political, and eschatological framework of the reign of God. Hence, the process of "emerging" involves a holistic process of formation as well as transformation. *Formation* is gradual growth and maturation; *transformation* is a process involving radical change and crisis, often characterized as *conversion*, which leads to the reorienting of the faith and life of persons as well as communities. Needless to say, formation and transformation are interwoven in life situations and the church's educational ministry sponsors human emergence in both ways.[5]

"In the light of the reign of God." While there are many visions of human emergence, the view of educational ministry expressed in this chapter points to the ethical, political, and eschatological vision of the commonwealth of God. The reigning of God is the key to Jesus' ministry. This symbol evokes the tension between the "already" (the gifts bestowed, human dreams partially realized) and the "not yet" (the promise, the longings) of God's reign. Further, this symbol challenges prevailing church and educational practices that foster domestication.

Only some of the diverse ways of actually structuring social, political, and economic life are compatible with the gospel. For example, in the United States the growing gap between the wealthy and the poor presents a formidable challenge. The ethic and politics of compassion and the "preferential option for the poor"—to mention a favorite phrase of Latin American Christians—thus become biblical-theological criteria for judging our political and economic system. Seeking and entering God's reign means that the gift, the promise, and the demands of a new creation being fashioned become the driving force of the faith community. Simply stated, Christian education must be comprehensively concerned with the fulfillment of the Great Commandment regarding love of God and neighbor.

Congregational education thus contributes to the *fashioning* of the new creation by sponsoring human emergence in the light of the reign of God in several interrelated ways: by making the knowledge and love of God accessible, while fostering human wholeness and care of creation; by guiding the process of formation and transformation in discipleship (following Jesus Christ) in the midst of the faith community; and by enabling people to participate and to grow in the life of Christian faith while supporting the church's vocation to promote faithful citizenship and social transformation for the sake of freedom, justice, and peace.[6]

PARTNERS IN RESPONSIBLE DISCIPLESHIP: LEARNERS AND TEACHERS

Christian education for liberation, justice, and peace inherently confronts the dominant values of contemporary U.S. life such as achievement, affluence, individualism, competition, consumption, and militarism to name a few. Christian education also confronts church practices of patriarchy, moralism, legalism, and lack of compassion. Indeed the fashioning of faithful disciples involves, on the one hand, confronting domestication—confronting compliance, indifference, or complicity with structures of injustice, oppression, and neglect. On the other hand, educational ministry invites active participation, in light of the reign of God, as compassionate, courageous, and caring citizens.[7]

TEACHERS AS SPONSORS

The teacher as sponsor is an equal partner in the journey of life and faith. Through teaching, actually coordinating and leading teaching/learning processes, teachers are engaged in compassionate initiative, hospitable inclusiveness, gentle empowerment, and a generous invitation to partnership and community. As sponsors, teachers encourage, make accessible the faith tradition, guide, and enable. This view of teacher explicitly rejects authoritarian, paternalistic, and manipulative practices of educational ministry. In other words, Christian education for justice and peace requires that teachers teach justly and peacefully.

Learners are respected, as Thomas Groome puts it, as "free and responsible historical agents" and as the primary subjects of their own human emergence. Learners are communal beings called to right and loving relationship with God, self, others, and creation;

they are also capable of sin and grace.[8] Biblical-theological and educational foundations point to the need for teachers and learners (and other church leaders) to undergo an epistemological conversion. Reality is seen more clearly, deeply, and truthfully as we focus on situations of oppression, alienation, and human suffering in the light of God's reign. We learn to carefully listen to the manifestations of the faith in the common people, and especially the poor, oppressed, victimized, and marginalized in both church and society. Suffering people often help us to better understand what is really going on around us—that is, what God does not want (lack of compassion, lack of well-being, and lack of justice) and what God does want (freedom, peace, and wholeness). Liberation theologians have underscored the epistemological privilege of the poor. The discernment and reflection stimulated by human suffering, however, must not justify suffering, rather it must lead us to confront and eliminate it. In other words, places of pain can become places of grace and new revelation, as well as situations of transformative learning.

GROWTH IN RESPONSIBLE DISCIPLESHIP

Assumptions in this chapter are in continuity with "reconstructionist" or "sociopolitical" perspectives on education: Education increases learners' awareness of the need for communal and social transformation and enables them to participate in such change. Most of what people know has been learned through active engagement and critical reflection, dialogue, and action focused on important concerns of daily living. Education for growth, therefore, is problem posing, working in dialogue with learners to address the problems we encounter in everyday living.

Theological reflection enhances these assumptions about growth. The words of Eph. 4:15, "we must grow up in every way into . . . Christ" are applicable to both teachers and learners. Explicitly embracing the divine summons mediated by Jesus Christ invites us to formation and transformation in conformity to the very life of God in this world. Teachers and learners partake in a process of growth in responsible discipleship that involves the *vision of the living God*, the *virtue of Christ*, and the *vocation of the Spirit*.

Growth in the vision of the living God, simply stated, means increasingly seeing reality with the eyes of God. By *respectfully attending* to God, to the world around us, and to ourselves, we begin to define what it means to grow in the vision of the living God. Respectful attending is another expression for admiration. We regard other people, and the often underestimated strangers and marginalized in particular with wonder. By knowing through them, we encounter the mystery of God.

As we *learn to use godly lenses* in perceiving the world, we see according to Christian sensitivities, with compassion, generosity, and a particular angle of vision. Scripture repeatedly shows that God often appears to focus on the margins. Of particular concern to God is human suffering and alienation. Therefore, through critical awareness, we *develop an alternative vision:* God's judgment and call to repentance often challenges tradition and conventional wisdom. In turn, our creative imagination is enhanced; we creatively imagine better futures grounded in the divine promise. Seeing with the vision of God is freedom *from* wrong ways of seeing and freedom *for* nurturing and evoking an alternative consciousness.

The vision of the living God, therefore, includes a utopian character, God's dream for us in the face of a reality of evil and sin. The key is learning to perceive, understand, and respond to the presence and activity of God in the world around us and in our own lives. Growth in vision is thus especially connected with the life of *worship.* Spiritual discernment is a way of learning to see deeply that includes the "testing of spirits" through the life of prayer.

Growth in the virtue of Christ as a second dimension of human emergence occurs when one is becoming conformed to the heart of Jesus Christ. The concept of *virtue* means, first of all, moral integrity and strength, or moral character. Virtue is reflective of the primary orientation through which we embody our beliefs and actions. Growth in virtue, simply stated, means ongoing formation and transformation of the person and communities according to the character of Jesus Christ. As we participate in the creative, liberating, sustaining, and renewing work of God in the world, we learn to care for the world as Christ did. The process of formation and transformation is lifelong. In Pauline terms, Christ is being formed in and among faithful disciples; Christ assumes unique historical expressions in individual persons as well as in faith communities.

Virtue can be described as our inmost dispositions and attitudes, that is, the "habits of the heart"—deep affections and passions that reflect adequate and genuine expressions of the love of God and the way of life according to God's commonwealth of freedom, justice, and peace. Therefore, as Stanley Hauerwas asserts, the kind of character we have is related to the kind of community from which we inherit our primary symbols and practices.[9] Virtues such as love, compassion, generosity, peace, justice, and hope may become constitutive of the identity of persons as well as communities. Experiences of these "virtues" are shaped by the practices and disciplines in which the church deliberately engages. In sum, growth in virtue thus understood means "becoming more human" with the heart of Christ.

Growth in the vocation of the Spirit means that we increasingly participate in the life of God in the world. Vocation is meant in a twofold sense: (1) "vocation" denotes primarily the call of God to human participation and partnership in the creative, liberating, and sustaining/renewing purposes and activity of God in the world; and (2) in accordance with such a divine initiative, vocation also means the human response to God's invitation with our total life.

From a Christian perspective, human vocation is not simply identified with one's job, occupation, career, or profession, even though those activities are important. James Fowler has articulated this understanding in a helpful way: Vocation refers to the orchestration of our relationships, our recreation and leisure, our work, our private and public lives, and the gifts, energies, time, and resources we steward. *Vocation is the focusing of our lives in the service of God, in the love of neighbor, and in the care of the nonhuman world as well.* Vocation gives coherence and larger purpose to our lives; it gives our lives integrity, zest, courage, and meaning.

Fowler further states that through a process of commitment, we discern talents and find settings in which those gifts can be placed at the disposal of the One who calls us into being and partnership.[10] To grow in vocation is to find ways of being and living in the world that are consistent with the purposes and activities of God. The theological notion of the trinity is helpful to us in understanding our vocation in the world: God's work is creating, redeeming, and governing the world. So are our tasks. Sallie McFague's metaphorical retelling of the doctrine of the trinity is especially helpful. She invites us to imagine God as (creating) Parent, (saving) Lover, and (sustaining) Friend.[11] Vocation, thus, can be associated with the tasks of (a) conceiving and gestating, feeding, caring, nurturing, guiding; (b) liberating, healing, restoring, reconciling, humanizing; and (c) being available/present, accompanying, empowering, serving, advocating.

Enacting the *mission* of the church in the midst of history is the primary way we grow in the vocation of the Spirit. In sum, we become "more human" by participating in the ongoing creative, liberating, and renewing work of God in the world. Discipleship and citizenship must be integrated. Discipleship contributes uniquely Christian content to the challenges of pertinent citizenship for our times. In turn, as John Coleman asserts, citizenship significantly adds certain qualities to discipleship: (1) it widens the reach of Christian solidarity by reminding the church that God's grace reigns outside its contours and that the community of faith exists *for* the world; (2) in the often intractable day-to-day reality of politics, it teaches humility so that Christian citizens learn the way of shared responsibility and solidarity in history; and (3) it represents a reality test, an experiential proving ground for Christian claims for this worldly, liberative, restorative potential in grace and redemption so that Christians put flesh on their hopes for a transformed future, the new creation based on the transforming power of Christ in history.[12]

PROCESS: A SHARED JOURNEY OF LIFE AND FAITH

Commitment to the ethics and politics of God in the midst of history calls for a refocusing of congregational education. Promotion of communal and societal transformation for the sake of freedom, justice, and peace is rooted in a prophetic and servant community of faith. Educational ministry focuses on social analysis, forms and expressions of power, the manifestations of oppression and suffering as well as the quest for liberation and justice, the role of interest and ideology, the dynamics of social conflict, and the possibilities and challenges of community organization.

Furthermore, an educational ministry oriented to social change for the sake of justice calls for an action-reflection-action process of transformative learning and teaching. More than a pedagogical strategy, change for the sake of justice provides direction for the very mission of the church in the world.

Educational ministry oriented to justice has three essential movements: seeing, judging, and acting.[13] While never neatly separated, these movements are key moments for the church's theological and educational process.

1. *Seeing* operates in the context of the real world, with special focus on human suffering and oppression. In other words, Christian education must begin with a careful social and cultural assessment of the situation. Further, such an analysis must seek to perceive reality primarily from the perspective and the longings of the persons who experience the lacks and the pain of reality. The objective is to discover and comprehend the character and the causes of injustice as well as to understand as fully and clearly as possible the nature and dynamics of prevailing conditions that generate, sustain, and foster injustice. When we see injustice and oppression as manifestations of sin, as fundamental alienation from God and humanity, we must seek to confront and change them. Assessment is not undertaken from a neutral stance; it stems from a commitment to liberation and justice on the part of all participants, including the will to be engaged in actual transformation.

2. *Judging* consists in the endeavor to discern the will of God in the face of the concrete historical situation. This is an interpretive task to be carried out both boldly and humbly, because we are seeking to know the mind of God (or, better, to discover God's dream). We illuminate Christian praxis by looking at concrete historical realities in light of God's own revelation—the Bible prayerfully reinterpreted afresh and the participation of the very Spirit of

God in the process—and the other resources of the Christian faith and tradition (such as church teachings on freedom, peace, and justice). This interpretive judging helps us find concrete connections between the present social situation and the gospel of the reign of God as those connections pertain to both social structures, as well as to personal and communal realities.

3. *Acting,* in turn, consists of exploring, implementing, and evaluating operational approaches consistent with both the people's hopes for liberation and the revealed divine will for human emergence and wholeness. From a biblically grounded view of knowing, truth emerges from truthful practice (that is, doing what is right in the light of God) and truth is also validated in that practice.[14] Christian education must include action and accountability.

Seeing is oriented toward social analysis, or understanding the world with a special interest in justice and the plight of suffering people, for example, because of poverty or racial discrimination. Interpretation, or judging, attends to "God's world"—the world as if God really reigned—in order to discover the divine designs with regard to human wholeness. In action, Christian education thus emerges from Christian praxis, "faith that works through love," leading to further praxis.

The process of transformative education operates in an inductive and dialectical fashion: Each step is closely related to the other two. Doing theology is a process of critical and constructive reflection (that is, seeing) on the practice of Christian faith in the midst of history (that is, acting) in light of the Word of God (that is, judging). In other words, just as commitment to, and involvement in, praxis must occur as an indispensable dimension of theological method, so must responsible action be included in the very process of transformative teaching and learning. Let us consider concrete proposals for Christian education for transformation.

Conscientization. Originally developed by Paulo Freire and others in Latin America in the context of popular education with a Christian inspiration, "conscientization" defines a process of liberative learning and teaching for personal and social transformation.[15] Conscientization thus names the process of emerging critical reflection whereby people become aware of the historical forces that shape their lives, together with their own, God-given potential for freedom and creativity. The term also connotes the actual movement toward liberation and human emergence in persons, communities, and societies. In a small group, people in dialogical and collaborative ways share their stories, experiences, hopes, and dreams. Through problem posing, they engage together in critical and creative reflection on the real-life situation while actively seeking better alternatives guided by the gospel of the reign of God.

The conscientization pedagogy can take many different forms in diverse social settings while remaining as an action-reflection-action approach.[16] For example, in the context of an inner-city community where people face unemployment, conscientization occurs as a congregation brings the people of the neighborhood together to consider the realities of life they face—the closing of local businesses, the feelings of being ignored by city officials, and the resulting despair. As members reflect on their situation in light of the gospel, they consider alternatives for action and ministry. One particular church created a community organization, a tutoring program, and a job training program for the neighborhood. As people continue to celebrate their actions in worship, they can together seek to see, embody, and live in light of God's dream. In another community the problems are different, but the process of engaging life through seeing, judging, and acting occurs.

Education for Peace and Justice. Due to numerous prevailing conditions that generate and exacerbate poverty, marginality, and alienation among people, Christian education as a means of achieving transformation both personally and socially is inherently oriented to justice and peace. More specifically, such an education favors the "curriculum of service" including, in Maria Harris's terms, social care, social ritual, social empowerment, and social legislation.[17] Indeed, a number of methodologies have been developed and designed to explicitly undergird and strengthen such curriculum of *diakonia* (service).

Kathleen and James McGinnis have designed resources to be used in educating and parenting for peace and justice. They assume that lifestyle, the method of education, and the content of that education cannot be separated.[18] They provide resources by which people can become aware of the cognitive and affective values that orient living as well as recognizing how change can take place through nurturing a disposition of solidarity with the hurting.

They argue that education for peace and justice is a conversion process, an education of the heart, a spiritual vocation where we are "touched" by the victims of injustice as well as the advocates of justice, and are supported by a discipling and caring faith community. Education prepares us for, and occurs in, the context of action—"works of mercy and justice"—as we engage in local and global issues (e.g., hunger) within the home or school, as well as in the community. In particular, learning through parenting is one of the first places to encounter peace and justice.

Transformative Bible Study. One of the welcome contributions stemming from Latin American grassroots religious communities is that the Bible can become a mirror through which the faithful will see their reality reflected. As people join together prayerfully and humbly in the framework of a worshipful, interpreting faith community, that is responsibly committed to the ethics and politics of God, they ask how particular biblical texts can help them understand their realities and call them into faithful action. They see and hear deeply God's Word afresh.[19]

For those of us in North America, a deliberate and disciplined change in vantage point and perspective often must take place. This change can occur when we seek to be informed by, and in dialogue with, people who are very different from ourselves, especially the strangers, the marginalized, and the victims of our structures of sexism, racism, classism, and ageism. As we engage the way these people will read the biblical text and see its implications for their lives, we are called to uncover the lenses through which we live and to expand the ways we see God acting in the world.

The process of transformative Bible study is thus facilitated by an ongoing dynamic interplay involving the real-life situation, the biblical text, and the context of the ministry of the faith community. Each of the three partners in conversation is indispensable in truthfully discerning God's will and responding faithfully to God's will in the real world. We seek explicitly to read the Bible in light of our current experience, the experiences of others, and our efforts to live faithfully.

Willful Contextual Dislocations. Another teaching-learning strategy for social change consists in two complementary movements of "going and seeing" and "welcoming." Through such involvement we reveal our cultural and ideological captivities as well as open ourselves to transformative action.

For example, travel seminars illustrate "going and seeing" as a pedagogical strategy. Participants are immersed in the culture of a Third World country or in the inner city through in-depth interaction with ordinary folk as well as with key religious and political leaders. Service projects for youth or adults are a variation of this approach. The educational design includes systematic research and reflection using the see-judge-act method. Participants must commit themselves to covenants of preparation, live simply with their hosts, and communicate to other participants what they experienced and learned when they return home. This approach encourages people to leave their comfort zones and become vulnerable within the contexts of poverty and oppression. Each seminar seeks to provide powerful experiences that lead to significant changes of perception and perspective, as well as cultural and political appraisal and orientation. Seminar participation also seeks to foster the Christian vocation of service in the larger society.

In this category of service in the larger society we can include a variety of *listening projects* consisting in structured visits to a given neighborhood or community; they are specific endeavors of "going and seeing/hearing" that are potentially transformative in themselves and, at the very least, are an introduction to further education *for* mission and *in* mission, and for possible collaboration within the community to which the church belongs.

The intentional practice of "welcoming," of openly inviting and receiving into the faith community those people who are marginalized in American society, those who are refugees, or those who are otherwise victimized and oppressed, can be another instance of contextual dislocation. Two interrelated conditions, however, are implied. For one thing, the church community must move beyond the gestures of charity and assistance in attending to the physical, relational, and spiritual condition of those persons being welcomed and move toward also confronting the justice and political dimensions of the issues involved, such as the questions of status of illegal immigrants, jobs and the welfare system, education, housing, health care, and so on. Second, the welcoming community will be expected to allow itself to be reshaped and even converted by the presence and participation of those "strangers" becoming real "neighbors" in their midst. The very life of a congregation and its practices of ministry, patterns of worship, and mission may be fundamentally challenged and transformed.

Other strategies combine the "going" and the "welcoming," for example, in planned and focused encounters between middle-class and low-income groups. Such encounters require careful preparation so as to ensure a climate of trust and respect; they must include sharing and listening to stories and actually entering into people's realities by visiting homes or sharing experiences such as meals, fellowship, entertaining, worship and other types of services, and working on common projects.[20]

CONTEXT: THE COMPASSIONATE CHURCH AND ITS MINISTRY

The church is the primary context for transformative learning and growth in faith as well as for communal and societal change in the direction of the ethics and politics of God. Congregational education calls for ministry to be perceived, oriented, and evaluated in the light of the gospel of the reign of God. Education involves the life of the congregation, that is, worship, community, and mission. Christian education enables for *worship* (lived and viewed primarily as acknowledgment and celebration of God's reign); it equips for *community* (concretely living as God's family and society); and it empowers for *mission* (announcement and advancement of God's reign through presence, deeds, and words).

The story of the Reba Place congregation at the beginning of this chapter illustrates the church as primary context for Christian education for transformation. The faith community can actually become such a place of divine and human compassion. The church is called to become an authentic living sign of God's love in the world and for the sake of the world. In the tradition of the call and promise to Abram—"in you all the families of the earth shall be blessed" (Gen. 12:3)—the church assumes a special partnership in the humanization of all persons and social life, which is ultimately God's gift. Christian faith communities seek to concretely embody life according to God's dream of the commonwealth of love, freedom, justice, and peace. In our North American context, such embodiments are bound to be different than the American capitalist economic system and those supporting values and practices that are contrary to the purposes and the work of the Spirit of God in history.

Congregations are *called to become revelation*, that is, sacramental communities in the sense of truthful, living symbols, and signs of divine love. As truthful revelation, faith communities are especially equipped and empowered to be fruitful settings for Christian education. They provide grace-filled glimpses of life in the light of the reign of God.

In the prevailing conditions of injustice and dehumanization, the way of faithfulness to the ethics and the politics of God leads the church to become an alternative, a compassionately inclusive community with a countercultural consciousness—in the words of Jesus, "salt of the earth . . . light of the world" (Matt. 5:13-14), whom Jesus has "sent into the world" (John 17:18).

As forcefully presented in the work and reflection of Suzanne Toton, Christian education for transformation consists of becoming skilled in recognizing the fashioning of justice, peace, love, and hope in our midst. We must thus enter into solidarity with specific communities of suffering and resistance.[21] Solidarity and partnership with those communities by divine grace offers much hope for us to stand and work at the frontier where God is also at work making all things new. The prophetic and utopian stance characteristic of the teaching of Jesus nurtures and evokes a conscious alternative to the dominant culture and the conventional wisdoms of our times. That countercultural consciousness serves to unveil and to dismantle the prevailing mind-set and to energize and empower the faith community in the promise and hope for a better world toward which they may choose to move. The community of faith must attend to human life and seek the integration of the religious, social, cultural, economic, and political dimensions on behalf of justice and fullness of life *(shalom)*. That kind of global project, needless to say, necessitates a common life and ministry—especially the educational ministry—to support the church's call to become an alternative way of seeing life and reality (the *vision of the living God*), an alternative way of being (the *virtue of Christ*), and an alternative way of living (the *vocation of the Spirit*).

FOR FURTHER READING

Evans, Alice Frazier, Robert A. Evans, and William Bean Kennedy, eds. *Pedagogies for the Non-Poor*. Maryknoll, N.Y.: Orbis Books, 1987.

Freire, Paulo. *Pedagogy of Hope: Reliving Pedagogy of the Oppressed*, trans. Robert R. Barr. New York: Continuum, 1995.

Moore, Allen J. *Religious Education as Social Transformation*. Birmingham, Ala.: Religious Education Press, 1989.

Preiswerk, Matias. *Educating in the Living Word: A Theoretical Framework for Christian Education*. Maryknoll, N.Y.: Orbis Books, 1987.

Schipani, Daniel S. *Religious Education Encounters Liberation Theology*. Birmingham, Ala.: Religious Education Press, 1988.

Schlabach, Gerald W., *And Who Is My Neighbor?: Poverty, Privilege, and the Gospel of Christ*. Scottdale, Penn.: Herald Press, 1990.

Toton, Suzanne C., *Educating Toward a Politically Responsible Church*. Maryknoll, N.Y.: Orbis Books, 1996.

3
The Faith Community

ROBERT T. O'GORMAN

"All these things were shared, part of community life, not a rare isolated joy, like reading poems. These moments belonged to a *people*, not to oneself. It was a ghetto, undeniably. But not a bad ghetto to grow up in."[1] Garry Wills in "Memories of a Catholic Boyhood" captures parish life as most U.S. Catholics experienced it in the middle of the twentieth century—a community of faith with direct face-to-face relationships.

The parochial school with its array of supporting structures made the community of faith a reality. These structures included PTAs, Mothers' clubs, Fathers' clubs, sports programs, altar boy societies, choirs, cafeteria workers, fund-raisers. Together the school, church, and parish life created a community in which one learned to be and live as Catholic. Values taught in the school were reinforced in the home. "Sister's word" was an authority often appealed to in family discussions. To not connect with the school was tantamount to not being a member of the parish—not really being a Catholic.

Protestant and Jewish communities in North America experienced a similar integrated structure as churches, families, and communities united to teach values. Family, school, and church worked together as an ecology of faith and education. Today how do we teach and learn through the community of faith?

The Catholic parish was a community that provided unmediated face-to-face relationships. In the 1960s, 1970s, and 1980s, however, the influence of these communities lessened significantly. Saint Robert Roman Catholic Parish on the edge of a city center in a Midwestern urban area is an example.[2] Founded during World War II, it was initially populated by young families. From its founding until 1988, the parishioners lived under three distinctive pastorates and eras.

The first, the period of youthful growth, witnessed a bonding of neighborhood and parish—through large families, youth programs (social, sport, and religious), and a burgeoning Catholic school. Building a parish identity and laying the foundations for what it meant to be a Catholic were the initial agenda. The first task to which everyone put energy was construction of a permanent schoolhouse.

Period two began with the appointment of the diocese's chancellor as pastor—which brought recognition that this parish was destined to be the "flagship" of the diocese. During this establishment phase, building the parish plant to support the school (a magnificent church structure reflecting the pre-Vatican II mentality of a triumphal Christendom) and the rectory were the tasks. The actual physical layout of the nine acres of the parish property embodied the educational vision of the parish. At the north end of the property was the rectory where the chief teacher of the parish, the pastor, lived. Covered passageways connected the rectory to the church and the church to the school. In the church, the child entered the parish life through baptism. Classrooms closest to the church were reserved for the younger children. As children grew older, they moved south through the building toward the sports fields and beyond the boundaries of the parish plant. In various parts of the school were the cafeteria and other meeting places for the after-school gatherings of the parish. The parish plant literally was a curriculum that informed people of the proper place one is to take in life at various stages of development.

Phase three is the story of triumph not achieved. The city's response to integration and urban growth during the 1960s affected this part of the city and its religious congregations. Housing projects went up on the edge of the parish and a multilane beltway dissecting the parish just to the south of the church grounds was proposed. The school experienced a downturn in enrollment. Because of many factors (including the age and mentality of the pastor, the fortress condition of the parish vis-à-vis the neighborhood, and declining growth), the congregation did not carry out the vision of the Second Vatican Council. One parishioner characterized the people of the parish during the years of this third period as "long-suffering."

The present parishioners are a congregation that has experienced disruption, upheaval, and a loss of community life, especially the fading of the parochial school as the central and dominant structure mediating secular and Catholic culture. Aware of these losses, parishioners have subscribed to an intensive process of education, the Renew Program that began in the late 1980s. This program suggests that parishioners meet in small groups of fifteen or so in an educational format where experience is joined with tradition and scripture in faith reflection. Here education is centered on the "present realities" of the people—concerns about drugs, crime, marital strife, job loss, and so forth.

Among these parishioners were emerging new leaders, several of whom had recently moved to the parish in order to be in an urban neighborhood. In the midst of this renewal, a new pastor came to St. Robert with a hope for parish reinvigoration and the generation of renewed community. He made the liturgy more contemporary. He restructured parish governance, established a new council structure, and encouraged the Renew process. He commissioned a study of the parish's educational needs to provide the "grist" for a pastoral plan.

This chapter examines the contemporary search for community in our churches and its effect on educational strategies, which the life of St. Robert Parish illustrates. This search for community has become increasingly difficult because of modernity's encouragement of excessive individuality. Individualism has shaped the educational approaches we have developed. This chapter proposes that community as the expression for authentic human development needs to be reborn to heal the atomizing of the human experience. Education embodying a sense of community reinforces both the development of community and the rediscovery of the spiritual.

The following questions guide this chapter:

- *What is the essence of community and how does modern life in North America mitigate it?*
- *How does the Latin American experience of church, as expressed in the base community, help us engage the ecclesial and educational tasks of creating, fostering, and maintaining communion (a "priestly" task),*

articulating and interpreting the learning of the community for these times (a "teaching" task), and caring for the needs of the parish, surrounding community, and the larger society (a "ministe-rial" task)?

- *What type of leadership is necessary to generate the types of churches and educational systems that will result in a community that affects societal structures?*

THE PROBLEM: THE NEED FOR COMMUNITY

The sense of community in the U.S. is less stable than in earlier years. We are more concerned with the individual. We lead more anonymous lives. A breakdown of traditional support structures points to the need welling up in us, the need for connection—through community and spirituality. Robert Wuthnow character-izes our late-twentieth-century relations as "allowing us to bond easily but to break our attachments with equivalent ease."[3] The new bonding norms for community are: come if you have time, talk if you feel like it, respect everyone's opinion equally, never criticize, and leave if you become dissatisfied.

These norms contrast with the old bonds of community, a social contract of family relations and close-knit community ties. Values and personal relationships are selected in an increasingly uncer-tain world with fewer authoritative grounds on which to make choices. Society's institutions, especially the churches, take up less of our energy. The traditional church fit well with the stability of traditional communities. New expressions of church will reflect the new forms of community we attempt to develop.

Because of this loss of community, small groups have spread like wildfire in the United States. Wuthnow tells us that four of ten persons in the United States belong to a small group and that two of every three small groups have church connections. These small groups now play a major role in our society—moral rather than political since they are private activities and largely invisible. The small group movement is altering U.S. society, affecting our con-ceptions of ourselves and, even, of God.

Small groups are becoming a glue that is holding our society together. They draw individuals out of themselves to share needs and concerns, make friends, and link to wider social networks. In small groups we transcend our self-centered interests, proving that humans are a communal people who even amid dislocation can bond together for mutual support. Small groups provide surrogate sources of intimacy and primary identity with a tolerance of diversity and emotional care. They address addiction, suffering, personal crises, loneliness, and self doubt. They help persons rebuild lives. They provide the kind of relationship that busy, rootless people can grasp without adjusting their lifestyles. However, small groups do not provide constant care as is found in a family. They do not provide physical or economic support. Persons are not related by blood and are not economically and legally responsible for one another. One's identity is voluntarily elected, not ascribed.

The educational heart of the small group process is storytelling: "In the telling of personal stories, members gradually become different people, individuals whose identities depend in subtle ways on the feedback given by other members."[4] This interdependence of identity makes us realize how profound community is and how community building is indeed a strategy of education.

The way that persons understand their relationships with one another and how they approach God are closely connected. In our society, Wuthnow points out, we have moved to a caring God. God is less of an external authority, more of an internal presence. Our culture "goes after" God, and the small group movement elevates this effort. Spirituality becomes utilitarian, making one more effective in career, a better lover, and a more responsible citizen. The quest for God results in pragmatic consequences: feelings of peace, happiness, and a good self-image. Spirituality is more concerned with helping persons adapt to the demands of everyday life than providing a sense of transcendence. Small groups then are redefining how we think about God. Thus the religious educators' attention to community is indeed crucial.

The small group movement prys us loose from the sense of community that we have lost. Nevertheless, does the small group movement forge the more enduring bonds that help us resist the fragmentation of our society? Wuthnow concludes that the small group movement is facing critical choices: (1) to stay at the comfort level of enhancing the lives of individuals (and fail to address the atomization of society), or (2) to serve the wider community. This crossroads of community development is an agenda facing religious educators. This chapter aims to move us to the second option.

GOALS OF RELIGIOUS EDUCATION

Two theological resources provide religious educators a means of looking at community and education for the church today. They are *liberation theology* from the Latin American church as expressed in basic ecclesial communities, and *creation theology.* Liberation theology offers us a new lived theology of community. Creation-centered theology offers us a new cosmology by which to view community.

Community life has undergone significant shifts in Latin America in the past thirty years. Rapid changes have produced major dislocations. Modernity has come full force resulting in the immediate and keenly felt loss of community.

In the crisis resulting from this disrupted way of life, recapturing community has become a necessity. One primary vehicle has been through a new form of church—the BEC (Basic Ecclesial Community). In a typical BEC, twenty members meet weekly to read the gospel, to pray and celebrate, to share their lives, to reflect on everyday realities, and to plan for their future. Two countries in particular, Brazil and Chile, have been in the forefront of the development of this new form of church. In Brazil, the repression of the military government in the 1960s brought about many gatherings in small groups for the purpose of prayer and protest. Today as many as one hundred thousand communities are active in Brazil alone.[5]

In recent years, Christian scholars have looked to Latin America as the most significant locus for change in the church.[6] Since the late 1950s Latin American liberation theologians have been working with the people—especially the poor—to change their realities of political, economic, and social violence and oppression in order to build communities of people to reform society. Local residents of many Latin American countries have banded together, managed their fear, and worked to change their environments through small basic communities. They have been creating "church" in new ways and transforming the institutional church. In these basic communities, they have become educated, both secularly and religiously, and have been empowered to seek transformative social change. A new church is emerging. In these grassroots communities, relationships are direct with a shared deep communion, mutual assistance, commonality of ideals, and equality among members. Community is both the goal and the strategy of education.

In BECs, participants practice "theology at sunset." They relate the experiences of their day (wages insufficient to provide food, shelter, and clothing; no medical care; inadequate education; political brutality) to the Scriptures. Their reflection calls forth a response—an action expressed politically, or through seeking a change in the oppressive structure of the *status quo*. Their education is an interplay of knowledge-use and knowledge-generation, both of which use scripture to understand the situation and give it new meaning through their actions.[7]

The people of the North American parish, St. Robert, described earlier, have also experienced disruption, upheaval, and loss of community. This loss has stirred them to attempt reestablishing their sense of community. Unlike Latin Americans, it was not oppression and poverty that caused the loss, but the hazards of overdevelopment (i.e., ease of mobility, independence, the anesthetic effect of material goods) that produced their loss of connectedness.[8] In the face of this loss of community, parishioners initiated an intensive process of education, the Renew Program.

Can the small community gathering be a primary experience of church for North Americans as it has been for members of the BECs of Latin America? Can it be a means of connecting people to the larger communities affecting our lives? North American educators can learn from the BECs the "theology of present realities."[9] Experience will then have more authority in our education. This has profound implications for educational strategies. The key then is seeing the everyday with a new consciousness in light of the gospel. One goal of the community approach to education is understanding the experiences of our lives and addressing them through working together as a group so as to continue creating a more whole and just community. We learn about faith and life as we work together in community.

Pastoral agents (small group teachers called animators) were indispensable in helping the BECs to evolve. They helped the BEC become an expression of authentic human development. Through these people's work, participants engaged in a testing of their faith as it was shared. This testing led participants to experience a strengthening of their sense of community, and resulted in a sense of belonging to the People of God through sharing adversity together. Such a view challenges the prevailing form of community in the U.S. where small groups tend to manifest themselves as support groups for individual development.

Community, as a goal for religious education, means three things: (1) a normative ideal; (2) reflection and support; and (3) a dialectic process. First, as a normative ideal, the community approach to education links both personal and communal development. For example, community development at St. Robert has sought to join small face-to-face groups to the larger tasks of the total parish and its role in its wider community. The small groups are environments to enhance the personal development of the parishioners who engage in them. In addition, the overall parish is actually a "community of communities."[10] Through their small groups, people reflect on their lives. Representatives of the small groups then become the governing body for the wider congregation as the realities discussed in their groups are shared and become the dynamics for renewal of the total community. Through the parish, the people in the "community of communities" reach out to affect the wider world.

Second, reflection and support take place through the conversations of the groups. Groups of peers reflect on the experience of their lifetimes in the light of Scripture. The leader's task is to animate—preside, listen, and enter the conversation. The meeting format starts with scripture. It continues through deliberating on the peers' experience, comparing and contrasting these experiences with the sacred text. The atmosphere is filled with the emotional bonds and sense of transcendence that develops over an extended period in a primary group.

Third, viewing the conversation about people's lives collectively is a dialectic process that empowers people to reengage in community building. Through the conversations, parishioners highlight the differences among their present experience, their hopes for the future, and the visions of the faith community. These revelations provide the energy for moving from the already (present reality) to the not yet (possible futures).

Creation-centered theology undergirds these goals. Too often church communities ignore their wider connections. Community can be the private gift of a small group that isolates itself from the wider world. Through creation theology we are invited to look from the already to the not yet as the broader goal of community education. No small group is complete in itself, for we are not isolated from one another, but connected. The cosmic, societal, ecclesial, familial, and personal are interrelated.[11] The earth is not the place on which humans strut and stomp, but is in fact our self-expression. We are not closed in a seasonal cycle of death and rebirth; we have a responsibility for the not yet. Creation is generative.

From the new cosmology, we learn that everything in the universe, including people, small groups, and communities, seeks to express itself. Because of this creativity, new life is born. Creativity can be described as a three-dimensional process. As they emerge into creation, each person, small group, or element of the universe take on a unique identity. Yet, this emergence and drive for expression results in diversity that pushes us apart. Therefore, relating the identities and differences of people and groups in communion is a critical issue for community.[12]

Small groups, for example, have different experiences and are made up of different people. Each group has a unique identity. Different needs are met; different options for new life are made available. The groups take on a life of their own that separates them from one another. For the sake of community, these groups must be brought into relationship with one another, by sharing their options and enhancing their bonds.

Thus, community is *in genesis.* Community is evolving. In the focus on community as both goal and process of education we are seeking not its *recovery* (a return to the "good old days") but its *development,* community-genesis—a continued birthing. The educational task is helping persons develop and enact community.

THE METHOD OF EDUCATION

Viewing a congregation like St. Robert in light of community-genesis, the method of community education includes service, reflection, and communion. Since the early centuries, these three tasks have been identified and assigned to the church, and are also settings for education: *Service* is action to generate and develop community life to enact transformative change; *Reflection* is the interpretation of the word of God in the present and an articulation of our identity as Christians; and *Communion* is the creation and maintenance of the bonds within a particular church community, and among other such communities. An easy way to capture the dynamics of the community approach to education is by looking at these three tasks as the hands, head, and heart of the church body.[13]

Service is an expression of action, or making a *difference.* As action **(hands),** service connects to reflection **(head)** and communion **(heart)** in that the new experiences that service generates lead to new meanings and new bondings. The community becomes renewed by its experiences of service. The crucial service of the parish today is to generate and develop community life in a society where fragmentation is the norm. Service is the response to the human condition of loneliness. Integrating persons into the life of the congregation through collaborative and mutual patterns of community participation promotes authentic human development. With its concentration on human development, the service task of community-genesis is sacramental, that is, God is present transforming society.[14] This service dynamic, then, is acting creatively to produce new life in order to enact transformative change. Community education changes both the community itself and the wider society.

Service is defined, in this sense, as the acts we perform during the week: with others at work, at home with family, in unstructured encounters with strangers and colleagues, and through the ministries of the church. These acts become the experiences we bring to the small community for sharing and reflection. We learn as we reflect on our service. We learn about our motivations and the effects of our actions. In small communities, these acts are *shared* with others. They are *reflected* upon in light of the readings of the Scripture. We are conscious that others in our community and our larger religious tradition share in our acts and possibly even join in performing them in a corporate effort.

It is important for educators in the congregation to give community members an understanding of "to serve" that is not seen as an "add-on" to what they are already doing. People need to see ministry in terms of "how I am in the world"—my *vocation*. Service is not just something to add on, but it is a heightened awareness of what we are doing and how we fulfill our vocations as Christians. Service then is acting out of the "meaning" of who I am. For example, I address the major life issues of job and work status. I engage in care for both social and personal welfare in ministries such as pastoral care, spiritual direction, and social change and justice.

Reflection speaks to the interior dimension of community. Everything in the universe has an identity. Identity is the interior awareness of, and connection to, the past and future—origin and destiny. Reflection (head) enables persons in community to connect their present ordinary life to the past and the future, and to participate in religion (*re-ligio*, to connect the "ligaments" that bind people together as well as to a supreme being). Theologically, God, the ground of identity, is revealed in people's experiences (spirituality) and in attempts to understand and enact the Christian tradition, the demands of the gospel.

As the faith community (and the individuals who make up that community) reaches for the deeper meaning of its identity, the people reflect on Scripture and tradition. Through reflection and community rituals, they come to "say their name" as Christians. The individual and the community come together. Reflection yields the clarity of identity and a consciousness of our connections with a past and future that is larger than ourselves. Reflection is essential to empowering a person to form community and to relate beyond oneself to others, the cosmos, and God. Reflection, then, deals with major life issues such as searching for identity, and connecting faith and life. Reflection is embodied in explicit teaching ministries.

Communion answers the human need or quest for community. The universe ultimately is a communion (heart) experience. The universe, the planet, the people, and the parish have evolved in unity, as a single organism. Communion is a bonding of separate identities into a web. Theologically, we envision unity with the image of the Body of Christ. The church is a communion of faith communities. Each member has the duty to care for the unity and good of the church and to be faithful to the church's gospel, wisdom, and mission. The church cannot be the church unless persons and groups within the church are internally united with one another in relationship. This relationship or bond is love. The goal is harmony and peace that empowers people to reflect and serve, to seek to create new life together.[15] Communion is embodied in ministries such as the worship experiences of baptism, Eucharist, and reconciliation as well as the ministries of leadership and organization.

Thus, the community approach to education is a balanced interaction among the three elements of hands, head, and heart: service, reflection, and communion. These are united through the process of face-to-face communication and conversation. As we reflect within small groups on our lives and our communities, we build together new life and new communities. In the Latin American experience, the starting point of reflection is a person's present experience (present revelation) and stories of the people and of the community. The texts of Scripture and tradition are joined to experience to both enlighten present experience and to enrich the interpretation of the text. Then we return to experience by engaging in faithful service.

Community, and thus the community approach to education, is an active process of communication tied to action, reflection, and experience. It is not limited to intellectual understanding. Note that education here is clearly not systematic catechetical instruction. Primary emphasis is placed upon the discernment of present experience—both as the starting and ending of the process. This process is creative. The end is the development of the Christian as a transformer of community and society—the enactment of the reign of God. The formation of basic community is the expression of ecclesiogenesis through community, the birthing of new forms of human relationships that result in the further transformation of the cosmos itself. Through service, we learn about our vocation in the world; through reflection, we come to know our identity; and through communion, we learn about our connection to God, others, and the creation.

LEADERSHIP IN THE COMMUNITY APPROACH
TO EDUCATION

A social group, such as a family, neighborhood, school, or parish church may or may not be a community. For a group or organization to be a community it must be a developing system that promotes the authentic human development of its members.[16] A series of orchestrated actions meet people's needs by identifying and then addressing them. For this orchestration to occur, leadership is essential.

Behind the success of the BECs of Latin America is a mutual relationship among the grassroots communities of concern, the animators, and the episcopal leadership. The leadership effected a movement of the people from lay passivity to activity, established links between religion and life, and demonstrated the difference between just fulfilling obligations and being faithful, accepted, and responsible members of their communities.[17] Reform in the church in Latin America did not arise spontaneously from the common people. It resulted from consciousness-raising by religious leaders who helped people see their own concrete needs.[18] The leadership set the faith task in relation to everyday life concerns.

Thus, there can be no question that leadership is the "other side of the coin" of community education. When we speak of community, we have to address educational leadership. The task of the leader is to help birth the people's consciousness of their reality, and to facilitate the interpretation between present experience and the religious tradition.[19] The tasks of pastoral educational leadership are twofold: (1) to stimulate the conversation taking place in the small groups so that various voices get to speak and to share their life experiences, and (2) to empower the small groups to communicate with one another for the benefit of the total life of the congregation. This empowerment requires liaison work among small groups and the parish so that there is a continuous dynamic of communication between the conversation of the small tables and the conversation at the governance table (expressed in the Sunday sermon, in the monthly parish council meeting, and other congregational settings). Leadership is necessary for the communities to both develop and maintain unity, as well as to work institutionally for social transformation. Otherwise, the small groups tend to become merely self-help support groups for individual development.

As we seek to build congregations into communities of faith where service, reflection, and communion occur, we need to consider the following educational leadership themes:

1. The goal of leadership is to help enhance community life in a society where community fragmentation is the reality. At the core of this fragmentation is a crisis of spirituality that asks, What is of "ultimate concern"?[20] Through community education we move beyond consuming and acquiring for the benefit of the individual to realizing that we are persons-in-community, interconnected with God, others, and the cosmos.

2. Leadership is mutual. Community is characterized by collaborative and mutual patterns of community participation. Community education proposes leadership that is participatory and in which the participants are partners.[21] Thus, education for community takes in the whole context of congregational life.

3. Leadership for community specifies the structures needed to support people's everyday lives in community. Living in community requires a structuring that entails planning, the use of rituals, and many other means for clearly expressing the expectation for collaborative and reflective effort between the leaders and the people. Leaders and people together become aware of the forma-

tive power of the present structures in the life of the congregation. These structures are filled with meanings and teach in powerful ways. Leadership involves assessing meanings within existing structures and building new structures. For example, a congregation's efforts to interrelate worship, service, and small-group meetings during Lent could provide a unifying context for reflection that inspires people into service.

4. Leadership, at its best, is a transforming process, an educational endeavor through which leaders empower community members to support one another in finding meaning in their individual and collective lives. Leaders facilitate the communication of the church's message that encourages people to serve one another in community. Persons who live in community are transformed and enabled to live practical, spiritual lives, both within the secure boundaries of the parish and beyond in the broader world.

5. Since community is not an achievement but an ongoing process, the leadership must revitalize itself to ensure both continuity and change. Leaders must be continually challenged with achievable tasks and supported in their work if they are to avoid disillusionment and burnout.

Leadership and community are interrelated aspects of a process intended to enhance the spirituality (authentic human development) of persons. This process entails ongoing actions in which leaders and parishioners cooperate in structuring their situation in order to transform themselves and the world at large. This transformation empowers people to live practical, yet spiritual, lives in the community.

ISSUES

A community approach to education may be hard to comprehend when compared with the more traditional instructional approach. For well over a century, education has meant individual development. In contrast, the community approach to education is not just a natural process of socialization, but a deliberate process of building community. As people seek to build community, they learn about their values, their relationships, and the meanings that guide their living. They explore and engage their common vocations in the world.

The work of Paulo Freire in Brazil has made us aware that community education is an authentic method of education.[22] During this same time, following the renewal of the Second Vatican Council, the Catholic Church restored the catecumenate, the process by which adults enter the faith community. This process centers on shared life experiences. The new members, the catechumens, and their sponsors relate one another's experiences. They share together what this new life in Christ means. Thus, in the community approach to education, the evoking and sharing of stories become prime components of education. Narrative education and mutual learning need to be recognized as valid educational processes. Education occurs as we reflect on our life experiences in the midst of community and seek to rebuild the communities of meaning that affect our lives and reach out to build community in the wider networks of life.

THE EFFECT

A caution about community as an approach to education has been raised by Robert Wuthnow. Small groups are both the glue and the solvent of U.S. society. They have the potential to bring us together or facilitate our atomization. On the plus side, the small group movement supplies a sense of community and revitalizes the sacred for many people. The concerns about this movement center around the fact that community can be manipulated for personal ends, and the sacred can be reduced to a magical formula for alleviating anxiety. Wuthnow offers us the two options of: (1) staying at our present comfort level and failing to address the atomization of society, or (2) serving the wider community and standing in worshipful obedient awe of the sacred. Thus, the cultivation of the community approach of education demands that its practitioners attend to authentic community development itself.

We naturally learn by participating in the communities of which we are a part. Authentic, holistic, community education recognizes the power of community to form identity and vocation, and challenges us to reach out beyond our communities of comfort to engage the interconnection of people and the world.

The way in which people understand their relationships with one another (i.e., their understanding of community), and the way that they approach God are closely related. Community in the U.S. is less stable than it was a generation or two ago. Small groups are adapting religion to the main current of "secular" culture. Secularity encourages a safe, domesticated version of the sacred: God is there for our gratification, God does not demand obedience, and God does not challenge us to a life of service. Wholeness is not just the sense of completeness-in-ourselves; it also belongs to others, thus offering us an awareness of community.[23] As religious educators we have the task of responding to the need for community with a spirituality that, on the one hand, respects the present experience while, on the other hand, sees each person's experience as continuous. The religious educator has the task on behalf of the community of remembering the experiences of the past and the visions of the future. Truth is not totally contained in present human experience, but is a cosmic experience beyond the limitations of time and space.

FOR FURTHER READING

The Archdiocese of Hartford. *Quest: A Reflection Booklet for Small Christian Communities.* The Pastoral Department for Small Christian Communities, 467 Bloomfield Ave., Bloomfield, CT 06002; 203-243-9642.

Baranowski, Arthur R. *Creating Small Faith Communities.* Cincinnati: St. Anthony Messenger Press, 1988.

Griebler, Marlanne, and Felicia Wolf, O.S.F. *Keeping the Conversation Going: A Method of Community Formation and Process.* The Institute of Pastoral Studies, Loyola University, 6525 N. Sheridan Rd., Chicago, IL 60626; 800-424-1238.

Killen, Patricia O'Connell, and John de Beer. *The Art of Theological Reflection.* New York: Crossroad Publishing, 1994.

Wuthnow, Robert, ed., *I Come Away Stronger: How Small Groups Are Shaping American Religion.* Grand Rapids, Mich.: Eerdmans, 1994.

4

Educating Persons

MARIA HARRIS and
___ GABRIEL MORAN ___

Jean Donovan was one of four U.S. churchwomen martyred in El Salvador in 1980. The month before she died, she wrote to a friend:

The Peace Corps left today and my heart sank low. The danger is extreme and they were right to leave. . . . Now I must assess my own position, because I am not up for suicide. Several times I have decided to leave. I almost could, except for the children, the poor bruised victims of adult lunacy. Who would care for them? Whose heart would be so staunch as to favor the reasonable thing in a sea of tears and helplessness? Not mine, dear friend, not mine.[1]

How did Jean Donovan learn to choose compassion instead of favoring the reasonable thing?

In 1939, during a lecture tour in the United States, Dietrich Bonhoeffer was pressed on all sides to remain in this country. Nevertheless, he returned to Germany, and eventually to execution by the Nazis, taking one of the last ships sailing back there before the U.S. entered the war. During the trip home, he wrote, "Since coming on board ship, my inner disruption about the future has disappeared."[2]

What led Bonhoeffer to return to his people? What in his religious education guided him to make that voyage? And why did such a difficult choice bring him peace?

In both contemporary secular education and religious education the idea of *person* is central. Personal development or personal transformation is often assumed to be the purpose of education. However, some Christian (as well as Jewish and Muslim) educators would object to making personal development or personal transformation the aim of their efforts. Does a focus on the personal neglect communal activity or social needs? Does the aim of development or transformation implicitly deny the doctrine of human sinfulness and divine redemption?

The purpose of this essay is to view a Christian form of religious education through the prism of person. Our doing this is not a rejection of other vantage points on education. Instead, we are asking what is necessary if the personal is to have an encompassing role in the description of education. Clearly, in the secular education of the twentieth century, nothing takes precedence over personal development.

In relation to this context, religious education has three choices: (1) reject the secular view as idolatrous and offer a religious alternative; (2) accept modern theories of personal development and adopt them as tools; or (3) agree with the importance of the personal but retrieve a broader and richer meaning of the term.

The first of these possibilities is usually characterized as conservative. Although many Christians (as well as Jews and Muslims) view personal development and transformation with some skepticism, they are not likely to reject the idea entirely. They do think, however, that such an aim is filled with illusion and self-deception. The most common alternative to development is conversion. That is, personal fulfillment is not in our hands; conversion and redemption from sin bring about fulfillment.[3]

The second possibility is usually characterized as liberal. It puts great store in the idea of development, a concept that has come down to us since the late-eighteenth century. While Christian writers who accept personal development as their guide do not reject the biblical call for conversion, this latter idea plays a very subsidiary part. Horace Bushnell and George Albert Coe kept the idea of conversion but gave it very limited significance.[4] The result was that the liberal religious education in the first half of this century was criticized and eventually rejected for not being Christian enough.

The third possibility is the one that this essay attempts to set forth. A Christian way of life is placed into dialectical relation with modern learning. For example, development and conversion are related to each other. A successful working out of this intention goes beyond the limits of this essay and probably beyond this generation of Christians. Whatever tools we take up for the task are already well marked as conservative rejection or liberal acquiescence. However, some paths of resistance in both directions can be sketched out.

We will examine some of the educational issues that are described by the terms *transformation* and *development.* However, our starting point in this essay is the more fundamental notion of person and personal. In such phrases as "personal development" and "personal transformation," the term that can slip by unexamined is *personal.* And yet, there is no better example than the person or the personal for showing the relation between modern education and Christian understanding. Numerous categories in modern Western thought are derived in large part from Jewish and Christian sources: community, faith, dignity, responsibility, and other positive terms in our politics and ethics. The attempt to use these terms, severed from their religious origin, often undercuts their political and ethical power.

At the heart of modern Western thought is the person. So common is the word *person* that one might not recognize that it is a complex idea with a specific history. At the beginning of that history is the Christian discussion of the relation of Jesus of Nazareth to divine power. Throughout much of modern times, discussion of the person was controlled by two groups: lawyers and psychologists. While there is nothing wrong with legal and psychological descriptions of personal life, a full understanding of the personal must also include philosophical and religious dimensions. A Christian form of religious education resists giving over the meaning of person to psychology, law, economics, and social science. A Christian education brings out all dimensions of personal life.

A diminished meaning for person or personal is evident throughout much of the seventeenth, eighteenth, and nineteenth centuries when "reason" and "liberty" became defining characteristics of the person. These concepts ignored the complexity of the person and the relationships in which persons dwelled. In contrast, the twentieth century has seen the person come into new prominence. Lawyers and psychologists should be given due credit for insisting on the rights and complexity of personhood. One of the great bridges among psychology, philosophy, and the arts has been the enigmatic little book, written in 1958, *I and Thou.* Here Martin Buber focuses on the sacredness of the *relationship* of persons. Buber makes no secret of the fact that the Bible is the inspiration for his description of personal relations.[5]

The Christian idea of person originated in a Jewish context of response to divine power. The focus of reflection was the life, death, and resurrection of Jesus. This reflection gave birth to a philosophy in which each human being is a unique person with dignity and rights. The Western world still lives on this heritage.

And what is a person? Why do we recognize human personhood embodied in Jean Donovan and Dietrich Bonhoeffer? A person is one who listens inwardly and then responds with outward action. Two characteristics stand out in this description, and have implications for the relation of persons to other persons, including one's relation to a personal God. These two dimensions of personal life form the basis for the remainder of this essay. The first reminds us that as persons we possess capacities for interiority and inwardness—what is often called "the inner life." The second is that as persons we are necessarily related to other beings; our relations are not only social but cosmic.

EDUCATION AND THE INNER LIFE

Paulo Freire, arguably one of the most influential philosophers of education of the twentieth century, frames one meaning of personhood in his classic *Pedagogy of the Oppressed.*[6] There, Freire describes the power of a literacy that enables reading one's entire world as well as reading printed texts. Condemning what he calls the "banking theory" of education (placing material inside someone's head to be drawn out when one takes an exam, much in the same way that a check is drawn from a bank in order to pay a debt), Freire proposes "dialogical" education, an approach based on the belief that every human being has "an ontological vocation to be a subject."

Such a belief, that we are "called" to be subjects, is synonymous with the conviction that within ourselves, as well as beyond, we are called to be persons. As this belief has attained worldwide currency in the twentieth century—often under the rubric of liberation—it has had political and social ramifications, especially among women, persons of color, children, persons with disabilities, and many others. It has become clear that holding up "man's" liberty and values or the "rights of man" is inadequate, and that "man" in these eighteenth-century phrases more usually means privileged men or men of property.

But the conviction that we are called to be persons has also had personal ramifications, most of all in worldwide attention to the inner life. These ramifications are noted not only in the work of Freire, who directed attention to the oppressor and to the brokenness within, but in the work of innumerable religious teachers. The twentieth century has seen a turn to piety, to contemplation, to ancient ascetic disciplines, and to a spiritual formation that leads to transformation.[7]

As this has occurred in the wider society, educators in the Christian churches have returned to older forms in order to assist persons in entering their own inner realms more deeply, even as they have devised newer forms. This search for, and discovery of, forms (vehicles that enable formation) have enabled a concentration on the interior life. At the same time, it has upheld the conviction that while persons' inner lives are *distinct* from outward, social responses, they are never *separable* from them.

The first time we taught a course on spiritual formation, we suggested the participants make a commitment to engage regularly in some definite practice. We asked them to decide on a weekly set of disciplines that include at least three of the following:

- *twenty minutes of daily prayer, meditation, contemplation or silent stillness;*
- *one day a week where you refrain from using a car;*
- *one day a week where you go without one meal;*
- *fifteen minutes of journal writing at least three times a week;*
- *one day a week of genuine Sabbath.*

We also suggested that while the participants were to decide on a weekly spiritual discipline based on the above, they should plan to come together weekly with a group of like-minded people in order to reflect on each one's practice. We suggested this because we had found from experience that although persons genuinely desired to set aside time for spiritual formation, they became uniformly strengthened in this desire by experiencing the support of a community.

Such a pattern for spiritual formation works well in a classroom or for a group that gathers weekly, although classrooms and small-group settings are only two of the many teaching forms that foster formation. Others include retreats, both directed or private; working one-on-one with a spiritual director; weekly involvement in parish or congregational prayer, worship, liturgy or sacramental life; membership in a social action group like *Pax Christi* or Amnesty International that takes time out for quiet, meditation, or contemplation as part of its practice; *lectio divina* or spiritual reading, especially on the lives of the saints, including modern saints; Bible study; and family devotions. The list is endless, and with care and attention, forms can be developed in any setting.[8] We know one local congregation, for example, that begins every one of its meetings, no matter which parish group is involved, with a twenty-minute reflection on the week's lectionary readings. No matter how brief the time scheduled for the gathering, this practice occurs first, and somehow, agendas are always covered.

Persons engaging in such meeting practices eventually discover they are nourished by three deep springs that serve as fountainheads for education and formation of persons toward "the inner life": silence, listening, and Sabbath. Although these three do not comprise an exhaustive list, they are nevertheless critical to spiritual formation and transformation.

1. *Silence.* As we search for nourishment of our inner lives, we must learn the instructive and formative power of silence. Like Quakers gathered in a meeting for worship, we must practice the arts of "centering down" and "waiting upon the Light" in the presence of one another and of the Creator Spirit, seeking to find grace at the center of our lives.[9]

One Hasidic tale is an instruction on the nature of such silence, recalling that when Rabbi Mendel was at Kotzk, the people of that town asked him how he had learned the art of silence. He was on the verge of responding, but then decided instead to go home and practice his art. Presumably, he realized that education in the art of silence does not happen through talking about it. Rather, it is a discipline learned through setting aside regular periods of time in which to move away from distraction and noise, even in the midst of daily activity, and wait upon the event that poet Theodore Roethke called a "sunlit silence"[10]—a silence where our ordinary ways of knowing cease for a while, and a kind of not-knowing or unknowing becomes possible in which we encounter Being itself. Eventually, out of such formative practice, the silence will spill over into our times of talk and conversation, permeating the whole of personal life as water permeates a sponge.

2. *Listening.* The primary reason for the silence, however, is not for the sake of the silence, but for the sake of the listening it enables; as we have written above, a person is one who listens inwardly as a condition for outward response. This formative listening work demands attending to the voices of wisdom; the pain of the world; and the possibilities for re-creation.

In Christian tradition, pride of place as a source of wisdom is usually given to the Holy Scriptures, both Hebrew Bible and New Testament, addressing to them the question of the prophet Micah, "What does the LORD require of you?" (6:8) and waiting in the silence to discern the ways in which mercy, kindness, and walking humbly with our God are to take form in our lives. If we listen not only in solitude but in community, whether in a prayer group or a weekly worship service, we can expect that wisdom will be found not only in sacred texts, but in the words of those nearest to us too, whether they are our children, our friends, or our mentors.

Christian tradition, especially in the example of Jesus of Nazareth, also directs the listener to hear the pain of fellow creatures, especially those most in need. "You always have the poor with you" (Matt. 26:11), Jesus reminded his followers, but he also educated them to realize that as long as they listened to the hungry, the thirsty, the stranger, the naked, the sick, and the imprisoned—and then responded—they would be called

"blessed" (Matt. 25:31-46). In contemporary spiritual formation, this listening has been extended to nonhuman creation as
well, to hearing the pain of an earth scarred by bulldozers, of
water poisoned by deadly chemicals, and of air drenched by
acid rain.

Listening must also be directed to hearing the possibilities that
exist for re-creation: of ourselves, our institutions, and our world.
One of the most ancient Christian practices, the vigil, is a special
form of this listening, which has been revived in the twentieth
century. A vigil is a preparation time of listening prior to taking
action in works that serve justice. It seems remarkable that among
Christians gathering today to protest nuclear arsenals, the death
penalty, the abuse of children, and the innumerable evils of our
sorry century that those gatherings are regularly preceded by long
periods—sometimes an entire night—spent waiting upon the
Word in preparation for the action that follows.

3. *Sabbath.* Because a Christian form of religious education must
always be in dialogue with a Jewish form of religious education,
we name Sabbath as a final component in educating the inner life.
The source and foundation for later rituals in Christianity from
contemplative silence to the Eucharistic meal, Sabbath has
remained an essential element in the development of the inner
life of both Jews and Christians for over four millennia. Even
more, as a necessary component of the Decalogue, it has
remained a command:

*Remember the sabbath day, and keep it holy. Six days you shall
labor and do all your work. But the seventh day is a sabbath to the
LORD your God; you shall not do any work—you, your son or your
daughter, your male or female slave, your livestock, or the alien
resident in your towns. For in six days the LORD made heaven and
earth, the sea, and all that is in them, but rested the seventh day;
therefore the LORD blessed the sabbath day and consecrated it.
(Exod. 20:8-11)*

This Sabbath command is ceremonial; it is also ethical, prescrib-
ing a concern for land, animals, children, workers, and servants.

None of these are to be *used;* instead, they are to be freed from work periodically, in imitation of a Creator God who mandated rest for all creation.

Such rest, and the inwardness it fosters, begins as a cessation of labor; in Walter Brueggemann's words, Sabbath is a "covenantal work stoppage." God's people are to rest because God has also rested; "this God is not a workaholic [and] has no need to be more secure, more sufficient, more in control or more noticed."[11] Nor do we. Ceasing labor is the way that human beings can carry out the first element in the Sabbath command: "Remember." Remember that God's world is not a place of endless productivity, ambition, or anxiety. Instead it is a place where listening to and receiving word and world precede our tending to them. Yet when we do such listening and receiving, in the regular rhythms that Sabbath and silence teach us, we are readied for the completion of our personhood. That completion occurs when we attend to those relations that are not only social, but cosmic.

EDUCATION AND OUTER ACTIVITY

Because "person" is a relational term, outer is not opposed to inner. Instead, the inner life has its necessary expression in outward activity. The deeper the inwardness, the wider the external effect. This paradox has been recognized throughout Christian (as well as Jewish and Muslim) history, namely, that the person seemingly removed from politics by prayer and ascetic practice can have revolutionary effect on political life. A Christian education, in addition to training the inner life, has to provide opportunities to serve one's communities.

In a Christian use of "person," the correlative term is "community." Persons who are mutually related constitute a community; and community is an organization that is constituted of persons. Whatever may have been true in the past, today's people belong to several communities. Many of these communities are fragile or fragmented; we might not even think of them as community. But each person has some few people who provide affection and a sense of identity; the people to whom one listens and answers are the sustaining community of a person's life.

There is a wider circle of people we listen to through books, television, and daily work. This community does not exclude the dead. Christianity has never limited the communion of saints to "the small and arrogant oligarchy of those who happen to be walking about."[12] A person can serve his or her community by listening to the wisdom of the past and passing it on to the next generation. Tradition means "to hand on," a process that every parent knows and every schoolteacher tries to join.

The widest community that the person lives in is the "biotic community." The human community has a distinctive role within the community of living beings. However, over the past thirty years, realization that the earth and all its inhabitants can be called a community has emerged. That is, each being has a degree of inwardness and is embedded in relations that have some mutuality. Human beings have a special vocation to represent the deepest inwardness and the widest mutuality.

Notice the difference between person and individual, two ideas that are sometimes confused. An individual is simply the basic unit of counting in a set; what is individual cannot be divided any further. An individual has no duplicity; neither does an individual have interiority and mutual relations. The social sciences, for their own purpose, deal mainly with individuals who, when grouped together, constitute society. While there is a place for statistical studies of individuals in society, the language of individual/social should not be mistaken for personal/communal.

In the twentieth century, the world tends to be divided between psychologist and social scientist. No educator can neglect the invaluable resources available in social and psychological studies. Nonetheless, a Christian who views education through the history of person and community will not take the social and psychological as the two halves of the educational map. As the inner life involves spiritual disciplines seldom allowed into modern psychology, so the overflow of that inner life may be into a radical politics and environmental activity beyond socialization and social conformity.

We noted at the beginning of this essay that much of modern

education is included under the term *development*. We also expressed the wish to engage such a term dialectically, that is, accepting valuable studies under that term while resisting giving over the Christian idea of person to one group and one method of study. A college catalogue, for example, would suggest that "human development" is a subject for study in the psychology department. Who assigned it there? Many people might be unaware that the modern idea of development arose in eighteenth-century economics. Psychologists came rather late to the idea. Psychology has contributed to an understanding of the development of the human mind; but neither *person* nor *personal development* are psychological terms. Psychology needs a context not only of economics but of anthropology, education, theology, political science, sociology, and ecology. Otherwise, development becomes a tracking of the individual and his or her thought processes instead of the interacting of person and community that is both lifelong and lifewide.

Jean Piaget began as a biologist and was fascinated by the emergence of logical and mathematical judgments in the organism. He never laid claim to a theory of human development; genetic epistemology was how he named his interest.[13] But given the almost total absorption of educational language into psychology, educators relied on Piaget and other psychologists for guidance in human development. The last half century has seen a series of resistances and corrections. Erik Erikson, for example, tried to add a social dimension.[14] Carol Gilligan, starting from a criticism of Lawrence Kohlberg, has inspired a group of women writers to explore categories overlooked or excluded in previous psychology.[15] This kind of correction has been helpful but the discourse is still controlled by psychology with a social dimension.

The work of James Fowler is known by most Christian educators in this country. Fowler's work is an ambitious attempt to synthesize differing psychological traditions and introduce what he calls "faith development." Fowler describes stages of faith whereby the person moves from responding to the authority of one's communities of meaning, to self-chosen values on which to stake life, and finally to a recognition of one's universal connection with all of life. Fowler describes internal developmental structures by which the person responds to faith and organizes content. This essay is not the place to offer a fair and detailed criticism of Fowler's efforts.[16] One thing we would note here is that after writing *Stages of Faith,* Fowler turned to essays on the vocation of the Christian, and involvement in church ministry. Those essays are also about development, but in a language not restricted to psychology and social science.[17]

The modern idea of development began as an opposition to Christianity. More specifically, it was opposed to what was presumed to be Christian doctrines of providence, grace, predestination, and final judgment. Conservative Christians are rightfully suspicious of development as a competing religion, a belief in the open-ended progress of the individual and society. The complaint against Christianity was that it presumed a closed world, created by an omnipotent power who stipulated only one track to follow. Development began as a form of social protest: Classes and wealth are not eternally fixed. A group or a nation can *grow* itself to wealth through the application of science and technology together with belief in the future. When *development* became a psychological term, the image of growth came along with it. The individual, free of religious restraints, can grow without limits.

The inadequacy of the image of growth is more apparent at the personal level. Death is an awkward reminder of the limits of psychological development. Every system has inherent limits so that unlimited growth is impossible. And a drive toward unlimited growth is pathological. Not inappropriately, our ecological problems are often compared to cancer in a physical organism. One part of the system celebrates its hypertrophy while not recognizing the damage it is doing to the integrity of the organism.

Growth became the metaphor for development because it seemed to be the only alternative for an endpoint that thwarts human creativity. But the metaphor of growth, taken from biology and mathematics, is too primitive for describing personal development. A person develops in relation to wholeness: The deeper the inwardness, the more integral the communion of persons. Of course, aspects of that development can be described as growth, but other aspects could be called *shrinking* or *simplification*.[18] A Christian view of development has no *endpoint* (what Christianity calls an idol) but it moves toward a definite end: the communion of all.

For the development of the person, a Christian form of education should provide two kinds of outer activity that complement the spiritual disciplines: the study of Christian sources and the performance of Christian service. Both activities are endless in the sense of not having an endpoint; both activities deserve to be included under education. Although in the past, education was sometimes too closely identified with book learning, educational reform should not disparage the value of study. Activities of service, once excluded from the meaning of education, may finally be finding their proper place as educational activity.

1. *Study of Christian Sources.* Having to assert the value of the study of Christian sources as part of any Christian's education is paradoxical. But previous practices make this defense of Christian study necessary. When the study of Bible, theology, and church history has been undertaken without sufficient context, the results have been discouraging. Either very little is learned or a narrow ideology confines Christian life and imagination. Too much too soon all but guarantees an insufficient context for understanding Christian teaching. The seventeenth-century Puritans thought that Christian conversion should occur at age eight or nine. The nineteenth century became convinced that conversion occurs in the teenage years.[19] Surely in the twentieth century we can see that Christian conversion, while beginning in childhood and developing in adolescence, has its main focus on people in their thirties, forties, and beyond. Conversion, in other words, is an issue of lifelong development.[20] Children should not be excluded from Christian education, but they should be slowly introduced into grown-up conversation where the serious study goes on.

An older age of the learners does not guarantee a broad context. Christian materials need situating in the appropriate historical and religious setting. Not all Christians need a survey of world religions. But all Christians can and should understand the New Testament in its temporal and geographical setting. Fortunately for us in this era, New Testament study has been transformed by new methods of appreciating literary and social context.[21] Many

Christians remain unaware of how intellectually stimulating such studies can be.

More study needs to be done with the history of the saints, but studies of individual mystics and particular spiritual traditions have emerged in recent years. The best-seller list regularly contains spiritual treatises; for example, Thomas Moore's *Care of the Soul* is an update of a medieval manual of piety.[22] The bookstores are filled with books on spirituality, but in many stores "Christianity" is tucked behind the shelves marked esoterica, New Age, self-help, and angels. To place Christian material into a personal context of today requires serious studies of our own past. Christians may need reminding by Jews and Muslims that study is a form of prayer, and that study is not an esoteric pursuit for a few scholars. Without study there is neither nourishing of the inner life nor intelligent directing of our efforts to serve the community.

2. *Performance of Christian Service.* In the Carnegie Foundation study, *High School,* one of the main proposals for reform is the introduction of a service program into every public school. A student should do service work in each of the four years; service should be required to receive a diploma.[23] This proposal has helped along a movement to rethink the relation of school and community. Many religious schools have a long tradition of incorporating service into education. For a church congregation, service should be at the center of education, the outer activity of prayer and worship. Along with affirming that service to one's community truly deserves to be called education, we would add two notes about the extent of one's community. As indicated above, the extension of community to any human being is justified; more questionable but defensible is the use of community for all living beings.

Christian doctrines and Christian prayer require a language of intimacy, not wholly intelligible to an outsider. This distinction between church and nonchurch is not arrogant or belligerent; it respects people's decisions to be members or not. Words spoken within a church should address those who are members (without in any way insulting visitors). This aspect of a Christian education is within the framework of Christian memory, language, and authority; an appreciation that is enhanced through the study of Christianity.

71

In contrast, acts of Christian service, while inspired by a Christian inner life, do not distinguish between Christian and non-Christian. When the service is a food kitchen, the relevant question is not "Do you accept Jesus as your savior?" but "Are you hungry?" Of course, in many congregations there are members in need of the corporal and spiritual works of mercy. Discreet channels of information should connect those who can give help and those who are in need. Although encouraging service within the immediate family is appropriate, a better test is service to the stranger in need. Both Hebrew Bible and New Testament leave no doubt on this point.

Serving the stranger in need is the biblical link of our connection to all humanity. Although the human race was already one when Amos and Isaiah, Jesus and Paul, Vincent de Paul, and John Wesley preached messages of service, never has the human race been so obviously linked as it is today. A leaking oil tanker or a poorly designed nuclear reactor can upset hundreds of millions of lives. Likewise, a gesture of friendship or a ritual of reconciliation can ripple across continents.

Finally, there is the "biotic community" referred to above. Like development, and perhaps as a successor to development, environmentalism is a competing religion today. It is where millions of young people find their religious experience. It would be tragic to have a widening separation and opposition between Christianity and ecology. There is a deep suspicion of Christianity in most ecological writing; there is also appalling ignorance of the actual histories of Jewish and Christian traditions.[24] A dialectical resolution of this misunderstanding will take generations. Meanwhile, people both young and old can be encouraged to get involved in serving the whole earth and can be helped to see that this concern is integral to a Christian view of creation.

Educating persons is a central task of Christian education. A person is formed inwardly through silence, listening, and Sabbath; a person responds with outward action through study and service that relates us to others and to the cosmos. The inner life and outward activity are intimately interrelated. Persons are connected to the deepest resources of life and persons are called to relationship, friendship, care, and justice.

FOR FURTHER READING

Egan, Kieran. *Educational Development.* New York: Oxford University Press, 1979.

Foster, Richard. *Celebration of Discipline,* rev. ed. San Francisco: Harper & Row, 1988.

Fowler, James, Karl Ernst Nipkow, and Friedrich Schweitzer, eds. *Stages of Faith and Religious Development.* New York: Crossroad, 1991.

Grimmitt, Michael. *Religious Education and Human Development.* Great Wakering, Great Britain: McCrimmon, 1988.

Harris, Maria. *Jubilee Time.* New York: Bantam, 1995.

———. *Women and Teaching.* Mahwah, N.J.: Paulist, 1988.

Moran, Gabriel. *Religious Education as a Second Language.* Birmingham, Ala.: Religious Education Press, 1989.

O'Hare, Padraic. *Busy Life: Peaceful Center.* Allen, Tex.: Thomas More, 1995.

5

Religious Instruction: Homemaking

ELIZABETH CALDWELL

The concept "instruction" brings to mind formal contexts for teaching and learning. Tables and chairs, desks and podiums, chalkboards and VCRs are the equipment that occupy the space. "Instruction" suggests content, methods of teaching, the role of the teacher and the learner, as well as the classroom context. For some adult learners, instruction focuses on the content the teacher has to communicate. "I am the learner, you are the teacher. Tell us what you know." For other adult learners the processes of teaching and learning are especially important. "What I learn and how I learn it are both important to me." The role of the teacher and learner are influenced by our experiences of being a learner. As the old adage says, "We teach the way we were taught." Too often we restrict the creativity of the teacher to traditional patterns.

Homemaking is an alternative way of conceptualizing instruction. The following stories of two classes in different contexts provide lenses for developing a different focus in teaching and learning within a congregation.

I faced a sea of faces in the first class session of a new course I had designed on pedagogy. Eighteen female faces across the life span looked at me as we began a ten-week course together. I began by talking about the syllabus and the content and process of the class. After I finished describing the readings for the course, I asked if there were any questions. No one said a word. That moment of silence has been faced by teachers across the centuries. In this case, I wondered what it meant. I discovered the answer throughout the weeks of the class.

We were building a learning community where teaching and

learning are shared. I explained that some requirements for the class were responsible class participation and student leadership in discussion, as well as beginning or ending each class with a brief worship experience. I led the worship for the first class and then class members were responsible for the other weeks. Finally, I explained that this class would make use of a variety of methods of teaching with attention to both cognitive and affective styles of learning.

I discovered that the silence that I heard in the first session was the silence of a strong *yes* from women who were hungry to learn from a female teacher and with other females. At that time, seminaries' student bodies were becoming almost equally balanced with female and male students, while faculties were less equally balanced. A room for teaching and learning was provided and together we struggled with texts, experiences, and visions for women as teachers in the church. Moments of liturgy in class became powerful symbols of the reality of the struggle of women to find a place in leadership within the church.

I had planned for the class to work in defining feminist pedagogy by the time we approached the middle of the course. All of the readings had been contributing to that moment. As we approached the time to define the term, the two students who were working with me in leadership of that particular class session came to me with an idea. They recalled what I had said about the importance of both cognitive and affective styles of learning and gently reminded me that the artistic style had not yet been used. They suggested that instead of asking the students to define the term *feminist pedagogy* with words, why not create a learning environment with art materials and invite people to express themselves. We set up the room and spent three hours creating, sharing, and making connections. We never got to the planned discussion of the reading. That had to wait for another class.

Several years later, I am still awestruck by the power of the moments of instruction in that class. I designed the class because I had some questions—more questions than answers. Teaching the class was a way for me to engage in an educational process with other learners. The class affirmed for me once again the power and the promise of teaching and learning where all are open to growth and change when they allow themselves to truly be present to the content, the experience, and the relationships with one another and the teacher. And it taught me that the role of teacher is expanded when the teacher becomes a mentor with learners and invites them to share in the mysteries of instruction.

A second story is about an adult church school class begun by two adults who wanted something more than lecture. They wanted interaction—a dialogue about topics that would help them make sense of their faith in the world. These two invited a few other adults to join them in this class. As the group met to plan, it became clear that members had definite priorities for the class. They wanted to create an environment that involved formal learning in a classroom setting as well as in the outside community. A high value was placed on getting to know one another as learners. It was essential that adequate attention was given to the processes of teaching and learning. They also wanted to have the opportunity for honest dialogue in a discussion setting. Curriculum choice was a matter of negotiation and planning. Since they wanted the freedom to "wander around" a variety of topics, they named themselves the Peripatetic Church School Class. Planning and leadership of the class was shared by a rotating group of members.

With great interest I watched the birth, growth, and development of this class that included adults at every stage of life. It grew from the original two class members to, at times, twenty or thirty people. Communal events outside of class often included family members of class participants. Celebrating seasons of the church year were special times to gathering together the extended family of the class members. Advent, Shrove Tuesday (the end of Epiphany), Easter morning, and All Hallows' Eve became occasions for celebration and worship.

Learning focused on biblical study, social and political concerns, and issues related to members' faith in the midst of the community of which they were a part. This group of adults were equally comfortable in both cognitive and affective styles of teaching and learning. I served as a curriculum consultant to the group and suggested one year that Advent be a time of focusing on the meaning of the season and on ways to make it more life supporting and less costly and consumer oriented. One session was planned for experiential learning by having members form smaller groups. I remember walking into the large room and looking at one group busily decorating their own wrapping paper by using the discarded ends of newsprint rolls collected from the local newspaper. Another group was busy making ornaments for their tree, and still another group was working on an Advent chain to help them think about the season in their life at home. As children of learners walked in, I heard one parent say to his child, "Look what I made in Sunday school!"[1]

These stories of two classes share common assumptions about community, learning and liturgy, methods of teaching and learning, and goals of religious instruction. Both emphasize the important connections between learning and a faith community wanting to learn. These stories prove commitment to the integration of cognitive and affective styles of teaching so that the processes of learning become like a seamless garment with methods so carefully chosen and implemented that integration is implicitly woven. The stories also reveal the dimensions of learning that are possible when the context, the making of the home for learning, is valued as an explicit priority.

GOALS OF RELIGIOUS INSTRUCTION

The metaphor of homemaking provides a conceptual frame for rethinking the goals and context for instruction in the Christian faith. Hear the voices of five educators:

In her book, *Peripheral Visions,* Mary Catherine Bateson has suggested that creating and nurturing the "vision" of a community is a "homemaking."[2] Sharon Daloz Parks has expanded on that metaphor: Homemaking "is a connective, creative act of the human imagination and a primary activity of Spirit. It is the creation of forms and patterns which cultivate and shelter life itself."[3]

Three other educators define meanings of home and homelessness. Think of these conceptualizations in relationship to present understandings and practices of instruction in the Christian faith.

Sara Little has said that "the 'homelessness of mind' characteristic of most of the twentieth-century world calls for renewed attention to the human need for clarity about belief, about meaning."[4] Letty Russell has noted that "Households happen where mutual love, care, and trust happen."[5] In *The Journey Is Home,* Nelle Morton confessed that "I came to know home was not a place. Home is a movement, a quality of relationship, a state where people seek to be 'their own,' and increasingly responsible for the world."[6]

Religious instruction in many congregations is carefully planned and required for children and youth. Adult religious education is an option before or after worship. If the congregation's model of education and worship assumes that adults worship while children and youth learn, then adults are rarely invited to participate in, or expected to engage in, opportunities of instruction and learning in the Christian faith. If the pastor assumes that there is no connection among the forms of curriculum—worship, community, learning, service, proclamation, prayer, and stewardship—then religious education becomes like a house with a long hall of separate, unrelated rooms.[7]

What is missing in such congregations is an ethos of a faithful learning community that empowers by its planning for faithful learning across the ages. Or in other words, making a home as a learning and growing community of Christians has been forgotten or abandoned. The church as a place of homemaking with a great room of people, using content and methods that integrate worship, education, mission, stewardship, and community is here never considered.

I have noticed regional differences in these commitments. I was reared in the South and worked for half of my adult life there. In the South it is routinely accepted that everyone goes to church school and everyone goes to worship. Churches of five hundred members frequently have six or seven different classes offered for adult learners. I sadly discovered that this was not a generally accepted fact for congregations in other parts of the country.

Now, living in the Midwest, I have noticed cultural differences in commitment to learning and growing in the faith. European American congregations have to work hard to get adults to church, making it as easy as possible for churchgoers to "get it all done in an hour" or certainly in no more than two hours on Sunday morning. When I listen to seminary students who are members of Hispanic, Korean American, and African American congregations, I hear stories about teacher training on Friday evenings, adult classes on Saturday evenings taught by the pastor, and Bible studies in the home on Sunday night. I also hear in these stories people who are hungry to grow in faith. For these people, the church is a partner in their process of feeling at home with what they believe.

Goals for religious education for adults in many congregations seem to be different from those for children and youth. Rather than curriculum planned according to developmental stages of growth on themes of the Bible, the church, and the Christian life, planning for adult education often seems to be market driven by popular topics that will attract adults for short-term learning. In larger congregations, adults often enter the classroom of a paid, outside expert, and remain strangers to one another and the teacher throughout the class meetings.

The quotes from educators at the beginning of this section address concepts essential to articulating the goals of religious instruction. Sara Little described a cultural attitude of "homelessness of mind." Adults struggle to make meaning of their lives in a world that grows increasingly more complex and violent. The first goal of religious instruction should be enabling learners to be grounded in a biblical faith that supports their making connections between the content of the faith and the way it is lived in the world.

Little maintains that belief systems help Christians make sense of the world. They provide direction and prevent aimless wandering around faith issues by offering adults the opportunity to engage in thoughtful, critical study and reflection on the biblical story. However, it is equally important for learners to make commitments to nurturing their growth in the Christian faith where they live and work.

Sharon Daloz Parks discusses the activities of homemaking and homesteading that work, as she says, to create a space "where souls can thrive and dream."[8] A second goal of religious instruction focuses on the environment of teaching and learning. This area should be a welcoming space that communicates to learners, "something is going to happen here." The space should also honor the variety of learning styles of the learners. Space for quiet and deep reflection is as essential in adult learning as space for "hard dialogue."[9]

The third goal for religious instruction must focus on the methods of teaching and learning that are appropriate to the content being taught. Carol Lakey Hess talks about conversational education that is committed to hard dialogue. Such dialogue requires commitment to conscious listening, responding, critiquing and questioning.[10]

A fourth goal of religious instruction is making connections between the content of the faith and the reality of faithful living. Such connections require, as Mary Catherine Bateson suggests, "a habitation of mind and heart." The faith we are attempting to communicate to learners is a living faith that involves both mind and heart. This living faith requires a learner to live between the reality of God who extends a covenant of love, justice, and shalom to God's people, and the world that has other values as its priorities.

Instruction for faithful living is concerned with two kinds of movement, as Nelle Morton has indicated: internal and external. The church, in its goals for learning in faith, must be attentive to the ways adults come to know themselves as faithful Christians.

Helping individuals, families, and congregations affirm their commitment to, and responsibility for, a Christian presence and witness in God's world is the external side of this process of movement toward being at home in the faith.

Religious instruction focuses its attention on the content of the Christian faith, the environment of teaching and learning, and methods and group processes. Religious instruction seeks primarily to educate Christians for faithful living, for finding a balance between the sacred and the secular, between the holy and the ordinary, between the sacraments in liturgy and the ways we live in response to our baptisms as we move out from the table where Jesus Christ is the host. Religious instruction must focus on helping adult learners of all ages frame their lives in terms of a new way of seeing, hearing, sensing, being, and finally doing because of their faith in God who is Creator, Redeemer, and Sustainer.

Homemaking defines the instructional approach of Christian education. By making a home, a congregation sets up an environment that provides for and expects biblical study and theological reflection so that through its witness and involvement in education, worship, prayer, stewardship, and mission, people move into the world as agents of transformation. Homemaking is a process of communal theological reflection. The educational process is holistic, and includes consideration of the learning community and the responsibilities shared by teachers and learners for the development of the household of faith.

THE TEACHER IN THE EDUCATIONAL PROCESS

Attending to the form and process of a group of learners places strategies for teaching and learning in a context larger than just content or pedagogy. The teacher of adults in the church is, first of all, responsible for building a space that values the integrity of the content, the learner, and the praxis—the implications of the Christian faith for faithful living. Sharon Daloz Parks has said that such a space needs to be one where learners are encouraged to be "secure, protected, related, nourished and whole."[11]

A colleague assigned James Cone's autobiography, *My Soul Looks Back,* to a group of students. The learners were African American pastors enrolled in intensive courses in a seminary degree program. For many, it was their first reading of Cone's story of pilgrimage from Arkansas to the northside of Chicago for theological education and his account of the racism he experienced there. After one of the students had finished reporting on the book, the professor sat in silence and decided to wait for responses. It took almost two minutes before the first person spoke. Two hours later, the students had finally listened to all who wanted to speak of their own experiences of racism. When the professor asked them about their stories, most admitted to having never shared these private moments of pain and hurt with anyone.

The students were curious about my colleague's response since she was the only non–African American in the room. She told them that although she was aware that Cone's story could prompt students to share their personal stories, it was the students' decision of whether or not to trust her, one another, and the learning process that made the discussion effective. She added that the first student who spoke opened the door for all to enter.[12]

Parker Palmer has said that "to teach is to create a space in which obedience to truth is practiced."[13] In the previous example, the space that the teacher created honored the contributions of the content she had chosen and the contributions of the learners in response to that content. In that space, truth was shared in the form of content, process, and reflection on experience.

A second task of the teacher is to consider the entire process of learning. An experienced teacher realizes that learning is a process of engagement with the content, with other learners, and with self in reflection on the call of the Christian faith. A paradigm shift takes place when teachers begin to focus on the process of teaching and learning rather than on the content to be communicated.

One of the members of the planning team responsible for selecting curriculum for the adult church school class that was described earlier in this chapter had been trained in group-process skills. This group member, Beverly, insisted that the class begin the church school year with two or three sessions of group-building activities. She believed that if learners were going to build trust with one another in a learning setting, they must first spend time getting to know one another. Beverly saw the whole picture of the teaching/learning process. She understood how good processes enable learning and growth in adults.[14]

A third task of the teacher is to create a vision. The homemaking activities of the teacher enable learners to think, to reflect on biblical content in light of their experiences, and to choose a way of being and living in the world in response to God's call. The teacher's responsibility includes inviting learners to move into new ways of thinking and acting. Maria Harris has said that "education includes not only the calling and the listening to the call; it includes the coming, the pushing and the flying."[15] An experienced teacher knows when each of these activities is appropriate with learners.

THE LEARNER IN THE EDUCATIONAL PROCESS

Consider the varieties of educational settings in which you have been a participant as learner, either in congregational or other institutional contexts. How often do you remember a teacher discussing the expectations she or he has of you as a learner? If religious education in congregational settings is to have power for transforming lives lived in response to the demands of the Christian faith, then teachers, educational leaders, and pastors must be explicit about what it means to be a learner.

The teaching in which I am engaged in seminary classrooms and in congregations shares a common feature. I make clear that I expect learners to be responsible contributors. This is accomplished by means of a syllabus for my classes. Final grades for the course take into account participation in class discussions. In teaching adults in the church, the first few minutes of the session are focused on sharing what will happen in the time we have: content to be covered, methods to be used, and expectations for dialogue and discussion.

bell hooks argues that one of the main goals of transformative education is "making the classroom a democratic setting where everyone feels responsibility to contribute."[16] Consider adult classes in congregations of which you have been a part. Why has passive learning rather than transformative education often been the norm? Why is it acceptable for the teacher to be the only one in the room with a working mind?

I spent a year traveling and training leaders for a women's Bible study I had coauthored. When I taught sessions from the book, I followed the teaching design that had been included in the leader's guide. The response I often received from Bible study teachers was "Our group won't do those things. They just want to sit and listen." The only way for the Christian faith to continue to be a transformative part of our lives is for learners to make a commitment to the process of learning. There is no one too young or too old who cannot be actively involved in learning for faithful living.

The learner's role of being a responsible contributor to the process has two dimensions. One is focused on what the learner brings to the learning process and the other focuses on the actions of the learner during the process. Sara Little's quote about the characteristic in our culture of a state of "homelessness of mind" relates to the first of these dimensions. Teachers, church educators, and pastors should expect adult learners to bring with them to church a prepared and curious mind and heart, open to learning about the faith and its meaning for their lives and vocations. Do we expect adults to read the biblical passages that will be read in worship? If there is an adult study book in use by a class, are participants expected to have read it before coming?

The second dimension of the role of the learner in the process is directly related to the kind of learning community that has been designed by the teacher. If it is based on a partnership model, then learners as well as teachers have the responsibility for careful listening and speaking. In speaking about the benefits of discussion teaching, C. Roland Christensen has said:

Partnership is both a window through which students can observe the teaching/learning process and a mirror that reveals them to themselves. . . . In deepening their personal involvement, taking responsibility for the quality of the discussion, and making an emotional investment in the outcome of the course, students claim ownership of their own education.[17]

Learning about and living the Christian faith occurs when learners are actively involved in, and committed to, knowing, interpreting, living, and doing the faith.[18]

THE LEARNING COMMUNITY

By offering long-term classes in the church school and short-term small groups in other settings, the congregation affirms by these actions its commitment to religious education for persons of all ages across the life span. While continuing these kinds of commitments to instruction, it is equally important for congregations and education committees to explore what it means to be involved in homemaking (the activity of providing an environment for theological reflection), places and times for learning the biblical story, and discovering the ways it can be shared and lived as we move out of our baptisms and from the table of the Lord into the world.

A congregation that is committed to this kind of homemaking is marked by the following household characteristics:

❏ 1. Honor for the learning space—This space is not confined to the chairs and tables arranged in an adult classroom. It spills out into every part of the life of the congregation. Learning is empowered by leaders (lay and clergy) who value education and are self-identified as teachers.

❏ 2. A climate of expectation for growth and responsibility—Church membership makes explicit what it means to be a member of a household of faith. Such a climate assumes that people have joined because they value the Christian faith and believe that their continued growth and development as Christians can be best supported and nurtured within a community of faith. Being part of such a community is transformative for both individuals and for the household of faith.

❏ 3. Mutuality in learning—This is best described as holding one another accountable. Carol Lakey Hess speaks of "conversational education" becoming routine within the congregation. Conversational education is marked by hard dialogue, depth of discussion, interaction from a variety of perspectives and questioning of norms and practices.[19] This kind of mutuality expects participants to engage, to listen, and to make space for one another's voices. A simple yet profound definition of religious education underscores the importance of this concept of teaching and learning: "Religious education creates spaces where meaning-making conversations can occur in light of God's presence."[20]

❏ 4. Experiential learning processes—We know and practice the value of experiential learning with children and youth, yet we often fail to value these learning processes with adults. Letty Russell reminds us that when adults "are only handed a message rather than encouraged to seek it out themselves through group story and action, they remain dependent on the messenger and do not learn to carry out the ministry of the Word together with others."[21]

Teaching and learning processes should be planned so that adults not only hear the content, but are equipped to respond in ministry in the world. Through worship, mission, and formal and informal settings of instruction, a congregation shows its commitment by enabling people to be at home in the Christian faith.

A visit through a church building on a Sunday morning provides an immediate assessment of the landscape of learning that is at work. Observing adults in class sessions gives indication of the nature of the learning community. One can quickly sense whether it is a place of "habitation of mind and heart," a place of homemaking where "souls can thrive and dream." Contexts for learning focus on both the explicit fact of space—its availability and the church members' hospitality—and the more implicit values of teaching and learning within a community of faith. Sunday morning church school is still a priority for many individuals and families. For other people, it is not the most convenient time for learning because of work, family, or life situation.

In the world in which we live, it is essential for congregations to consider a variety of contexts for adult learning: retreats; short-term evening learning opportunities that include dinner; breakfast gatherings for prayer and Bible study; midday Lenten worship and lunch breaks; midmorning coffee and conversation for parents who drop off their children at Parent's Morning Out programs; mission/work camps; or conversation during meal preparation at a shelter for the homeless. Each of these are opportunities for teaching and learning about the Christian faith.

Contexts are also influenced by the priority and value that a congregation places on learning and growing within the life of the Christian faith. Are teachers and educational leaders publicly affirmed, commissioned, and thanked? Are there training opportunities available for persons who agree to serve as teachers in the church? Is the pastor involved in teaching? Does anyone ask teachers about their teaching and how it is going, or what she or he is learning?

Letty Russell has affirmed that to say "I live in a 'household of freedom' is to use a metaphorical description of one's freedom to participate with others in a mutual caring, drawn from the concrete experience of the slaves living in Pharaoh's 'house of bondage' and then moving out as the people of God towards a new 'house of freedom.' "[22] The power to work as people of transformation coming into the world with faith that is remembered, retold, and embodied is enabled when learners are spiritually formed in a household of freedom and faith.

A FACE FOR MINISTRY AND PUBLIC LIFE

The church must support people in the articulation of their belief systems. The impact of the Christian faith on our culture continues to diminish as membership in mainline denominations declines and people search for meaning in their lives in a world that is increasingly more complex, violent, and divided between the very rich and the very poor. For Christians to believe that they are living in a culture that is predominantly Christian is foolish. Children grow up biblically illiterate in homes where Bibles abound but are rarely opened. We have become a generation incapable of passing on the stories of our faith. The face of our faith appears to be extremely impoverished.

There are several results for people receiving religious instruction in order to live a life of faith in public. First, through homemaking we "cultivate and shelter life," as Sharon Daloz Parks describes it. We prepare people to live with a face of faith in the world. That requires that adult Christians make intentional commitments to nurturing their faith, both individually and communally. Establishing regular patterns of spiritual formation—habits of mind and heart—has the power to feed hungry souls and form a face of faith that can meet the world with all of its demands and challenges. A congregation that is explicit with its members about the value of Christian nurture and Christian witness in the world can be a transformative presence in the community.

A second benefit is concerned with the models of teaching and learning that are used. When teachers are taught to think about context, learners, and content, they are made aware that their teaching makes a difference in the lives of the learners. Moreover, when leaders experience reading a context and are sensitive to dimensions of power, partnership, and mutuality that are present, they become sensitized to issues of justice and ministry. Teachers who work to help the learners make connections between the content and the practice of the Christian faith empower transformative learning.

If you were to ask adults what homemaking involves, you would probably get a variety of answers. Whether the task is fixing a leaking roof or preparing a nutritious meal, most would agree that a lot of time, energy, and commitment is involved in making a home. The same is true for homemaking as it relates to a community of faith.

The third benefit is creating a space for learning where "souls can thrive and dream," where a "habitation of mind and heart" is encouraged in the context of "hard dialogue." "Homelessness of mind" can be replaced by faces of faith when adults and congregations renew their faith commitments and their energy to engage the world. We tend a household of faith as a setting that focuses, renews, and empowers ministry. When we experience the church as a home of nurture and witness, we are propelled to offer that experience and vision to the world.

A psalmist has confessed that the statutes of God "have been my songs in the house of my pilgrimage" (Ps. 119:54 KJV). The NRSV translates "house of my pilgrimage" as "wherever I make my home." In homemaking, the congregation works to help its people learn the songs and stories of God so that this presence is with them wherever they make their home. Moreover, the congregation makes a commitment to send people out, blessed with the waters of baptism and nourished at the table of Jesus Christ. They go forth with a story, faith, and expectation for responsible Christian living.

FOR FURTHER READING

Groome, Thomas. *Christian Religious Education*. San Francisco: Harper & Row, 1980.

Little, Sara. *To Set One's Heart, Belief and Teaching in the Church*. Atlanta: John Knox Press, 1983.

Osmer, Richard Robert. *Teaching for Faith.* Louisville: Westminster/John Knox Press, 1992.

Palmer, Parker. *To Know As We Are Known: Education as Spiritual Journey.* San Francisco: HarperSanFrancisco, 1993.

Seymour, Jack L., Margaret Ann Crain, and Joseph V. Crockett. *Educating Christians.* Nashville: Abingdon Press, 1993. See especially chapter 7.

Vogel, Linda J., *Teaching and Learning in Communities of Faith: Empowering Adults Through Religious Education.* San Francisco: Jossey-Bass, 1991.

6
Assessing Approaches to Christian Education
JACK L. SEYMOUR and
___ MARGARET ANN CRAIN ___

Directions: Below are ten phrases. Choose the answer that best expresses your hopes for Christian education. Each phrase can be completed by using the four statements (a, b, c, d) listed below it. For each of the ten items, prioritize the answers using the ranking of 4 to 1 (4 is highest and 1 is lowest). Use each number (1, 2, 3, 4) only once per item.

1. The church
___a. supports and encourages people on their personal journeys of faith.
___b. shares the message of the Christian faith.
___c. works for justice and serves those in need.
___d. is a fellowship of people who seek to live the faith together.

2. Christian education
___a. shapes the congregation into a community of worship, fellowship, and mission.
___b. encourages individuals on their spiritual journeys.
___c. teaches the story and practices of Christianity.
___d. empowers persons and the church to care for, and work in, the world.

3. The church's educational ministry needs leaders who
___a. teach others the meanings of the faith.
___b. walk with others on their spiritual journeys.
___c. prepare people to participate in the worship, fellowship, and mission of the congregation.
___d. encourage people to work for justice.

4. The church's educational ministry assists learners
___a. in becoming full participants in the community of faith.
___b. in responding to needs in the world.
___c. in continuing to grow in spiritual vitality.
___d. in studying the story and faith of Christianity.

5. The content of Christian education includes
___a. issues and concerns of the world.
___b. Christian tradition and scripture.
___c. personal experience and spiritual growth.
___d. ministries of the congregation.

6. Settings for Christian education include
___a. small groups where persons are challenged to grow in faith.
___b. any place where we embody God's love.
___c. formal learning groups, such as church schools, camps, or study groups.
___d. the congregation's total life and ministries.

7. The goals of Christian education are
___a. to inspire the church and individuals to work for the renewal and healing of creation.
___b. to teach the beliefs, stories, and practices of Christianity.
___c. to enrich the life of a congregation and its ministries.
___d. to nurture and motivate persons to grow in faith.

8. Resources for Christian education include
___a. the life of the church, its rituals, fellowship groups, worship, and service.
___b. analysis of important world and community issues in light of the gospel.
___c. prepared studies that teach the faith and its relationship to living.
___d. the spiritual disciplines of prayer and meditation that connect life experiences to Christian faith.

9. Problems facing the church include

___a. learning how to be an agent of change and healing in a broken world.

___b. growing into a loving and serving congregation.

___c. helping people continue to explore and grow in faith.

___d. helping people know the meanings of Scripture and tradition for their lives.

10. The church's educational ministry succeeds when

___a. people place high priority on knowing the Christian story.

___b. people live out their learnings in ministries.

___c. people reflect on their lives in light of the gospel.

___d. people become a community of support for one another.

Scoring the Assessment

Listed below are the letters that correspond to the four statements for each phrase. Fill in the number value that you gave each statement. NOTE THAT THE ORDER OF THE LETTERS CHANGES. After the value for each phrase has been assigned, add the columns. A value over twenty-five indicates a priority for that style.

	Transformation	Faith Community	Spiritual Development	Religious Instruction
1.	c __	d __	a __	b __
2.	d __	a __	b __	c __
3.	d __	c __	b __	a __
4.	b __	a __	c __	d __
5.	a __	d __	c __	b __
6.	b __	d __	a __	c __
7.	a __	c __	d __	b __
8.	b __	a __	d __	c __
9.	a __	b __	c __	d __
10.	b __	d __	c __	a __

TOTAL _____   _____   _____   _____

7

Listening to Churches: Christian Education in Congregational Life

___ MARGARET ANN CRAIN ___

The phone rings. Michael, the Director of Christian Education, picks up the receiver and quickly recognizes Bill's voice on the other end of the line. After Michael and Bill exchange greetings, Bill gets to the point of his call. "Michael, I'm wondering if you could help me with my Sunday school class. We need something. I just feel like we're floundering. We have had really good speakers and discussions each week, but we run into theological disagreements and then we all just shut up. People are afraid to talk about deeper theological issues that are really important. I get so frustrated about the amount of time we spend planning our parties—which are great—while we need to be learning about what we should believe. What can we do?"

"Well, Bill," Michael began thoughtfully, "I'm glad you called me. Tell me more about what you wish your class would do." Michael knew that Bill had lost his mother earlier in the year. He had always been very active in the congregation, but recently he had dropped out of the Evangelism Committee and often missed worship.

"It just feels to me like we are always on the surface. Last week our teacher was continuing the series on the Gospel of John. We began talking about the Resurrection and Jesus' promise of eternal life. Someone said that she didn't believe in heaven as a place. Someone else said that the Bible is clear that if we accept Jesus we will have eternal life and he was sure that that was in heaven. I was wondering about my mother. I need to believe that she is with God. . . . But I am confused about what I am supposed to believe."

"Bill, I imagine that the conversation about heaven seemed very important to you. I know of a new study that has just been published that could help your class explore these questions. Faye Jones might be available to teach it. She is a sensitive teacher, and is well informed about the Bible. Do you think your class might be interested?"

This conversation clearly embodies the religious instruction approach to Christian education. Bill and Michael were seeking to enable the learners in that class to address the questions of their lives in light of biblical faith, guided by a teacher who would build a safe community in which to search for and claim new meanings. Bill expressed his needs to reflect theologically on the questions raised by his mother's death so that he could continue to live faithfully. He was clearly troubled. His changed participation in the congregation reflected the turmoil of his emotions. But he was seeking a community of learners where he could be at home and grounded in the content of the faith.

The next week, Michael received another call. This time another member of the class, Alma, was asking a different question. "I get so frustrated," Alma began. "I want to get our class signed up to work on the Habitat for Humanity project one Saturday a month. Through my work at the bank, I know that mortgage interest rates are high and lenders require a large down payment to purchase a house. People who are not making large salaries, or who don't have parents to help them out just can't buy a house. And then they pay so much money in rent that they can't ever save for a down payment. My classmates keep saying that these people should get another job. They have no idea what life is like for single moms or people with little education. I know though. I struggled to raise my boys and go to school, and I barely scraped by. I don't know how many poor working people make it. The Habitat houses offer one way for them to buy a house. I think we should help."

"Yes, Alma" replied Michael. "It was really an eye-opener for me when you and I worked with that family last year on their Habitat house. I was so moved by their excitement about their

94

new house. If I recall, the three children, their mom, and grand-mother had all been living in three rooms. Both the mom and grandmother worked, but they didn't make enough to save toward buying a home. I'm not sure who was more thrilled the day we dedicated the house, the family or me. I really learned what it means to be the Body of Christ during that project. I felt such solidarity with them during the dedication service. They taught me so much about families whose members love one another and work together. It was a gift."

"How can we get my class involved so that they can see what life is like for the families that Habitat helps?"

"We'll need to find ways to help them *see*. What if you invite the family we worked with on the Habitat house last year to your Christmas banquet? Maybe they could talk about why they think they were chosen to receive a house, and what it means to them. Then maybe we can get the class to agree to work on a Habitat project for at least a month before having to commit to an entire year."

Michael and Alma knew the power of *seeing* the world and its injustices. Working side by side with people who could not afford to buy a home without the help of Habitat for Humanity, talking with each other about how our economic systems can prevent the working poor from ever becoming free of debt, and reflecting on the call of the gospel to love neighbor brought them to a point of judgment. Because they had *judged* the systems that keep the working poor chained to a cycle of poverty, they wanted to *act*. They wanted to involve others in doing works of justice, seeking to move toward the reign of God. They were learning through the transformation approach to Christian education.

The other two approaches may also be represented in that same Sunday school class. Possibly, some other member of the class will call Michael with concerns about the community of the class. She or he will be concerned that members of the class do not know one another well enough. Members need to work hard at building a caring, inclusive community that supports each member of the group, but also is concerned and caring about the world. This class member may express concerns that the group is not doing a good job of welcoming a new member, or that they are not con-

fronting a member who is judgmental. Faith communities celebrate and grieve together. A faith community approach to Christian education would build a class that is so closely bonded that
each member is encouraged to grow spiritually and live a life of
service.

Still others in that class probably believe they are on unique
spiritual journeys. They "shop" among the activities and learning
foci of the class for those topics that address their current needs.
The spiritual growth approach prompts a learner to focus on an
inner life of prayer and exploration of the disciplines of the spirit.
These individuals seek opportunities to look into their own hearts
and lives for God's presence and guidance. The inner journey is
only meaningful as it results in a life of love and service, as Maria
Harris and Gabriel Moran point out in chapter 4. However, focusing on unique individual needs may make it seem difficult to
build community and loyalty in a class.

Meanwhile, in a small congregation in rural America, the pastor,
Sally, is thinking about the ways people in her congregation learn
to love God and to love their neighbors. They learn the stories of
the Christian tradition as they sing hymns together in worship; as
they prepare and enjoy the Christmas pageant; and as they plan,
teach, or participate in vacation Bible school. Each person in the
congregational community from the youngest baby to the senior
elder is included in activities as he or she is able, learning thereby
what it means to live as a faithful Christian and what it means to
be loved. For example, Sally and her congregation have accepted
their share of responsibility for the community food pantry. As
church members stock the pantry and meet those who come needing food for their families, they are learning about poverty and its
causes. They have invited their congress member to attend an
upcoming worship service, hoping to impress upon him the
importance of continuing a federal program that helps families
with children. The women's group has started a prayer ministry,
and has planned a retreat in the fall for mothers of young children
in their congregation, hoping to provide a time for these women
to get in touch with their own needs and to strengthen their relationship with God during a weekend at the lake. Others in the
congregation will provide childcare to make this time of spiritual

growth possible. Pastor Sally knows that many in her congregation would not think of retreats, fellowship dinners or worship as "Christian education," but she sees that learning and transformation could occur in all of them, and in myriads of other ways as well.

THE COMPLEXITY OF CONGREGATIONAL LIFE

Each of the writers in this volume has visualized congregations with far more homogeneity than they actually have. In reality most congregations, if not most groups within congregations, operate out of all four approaches. They are clearly not mutually exclusive. The approach we favor affects our priorities or the place where we want to start. For instance, the religious instruction approach emphasizes teaching and content. People operating out of this approach tend to begin with selecting curriculum and then recruit and train teachers. Transformation approach proponents tend to gather everyone together to engage in an action, such as renovating a substandard house, knowing that they will understand the impact of poverty better and be empowered to act to change economic systems. The spiritual development approach causes people to begin by looking inward, taking one's own spiritual temperature. People beginning from one approach may become frustrated with others who are beginning from another point.

In addition, every congregation is made up of people with many degrees of intentionality and involvement. While some are deeply committed and faithful, others come occasionally with little reflection on faith. Some may come for the weekday nursery school or the basketball team and have no commitment to the goals of the congregation itself. Picture a light source, densely bright and yellow in the center, but dimming as the observer moves away from the center. Those congregants who are highly committed are drawn together in the middle, tightly packed, resembling the center of the light source; the energy is intense. Out on the periphery, the people are farther and farther apart, less drawn toward the light and heat of the center, more inclined to disconnect. A congregation—large or small—is a gathering of people with varieties of purposes, varieties of needs, and varieties of involvement.

THE CHRISTIAN EDUCATOR IN CONGREGATIONAL LIFE

Educators in congregations are those who are evaluating, planning, and implementing opportunities for learning to love God and to love their neighbors (Matt. 22:36-40). In the majority of congregations, these educators are volunteers in partnership with the pastor. A few congregations have professional educators. But all congregations educate. All congregations need persons who reflect on how they educate and who plan and implement more effective opportunities for learning. "The church is only one generation away from extinction," may be an old cliché, but it is true, nevertheless. If we do not continue to teach people what it means to be Christian, the faith will soon die out. If you are reading this book, you are in some sense an educator and must take some responsibility for this reflection and intentionality.

Christian educators—whether lay, professional, or ordained— begin with the conviction that God's grace goes before us. Although every congregation often fails to live up to Jesus' commandment to love God and neighbor, every congregation also has an "already/not yet" character.[1] As we love one another, offer healing, work for justice, and claim our identities as children of God, we make God's presence concrete. The reign of God that has not yet been fulfilled, is, at moments, already present. This conviction provides the hope that calls Christian educators forward.

Yet, the congregations in which we work are living, complex, messy, and willful. Educators who attempt to decide on an approach to Christian education and ensure that the ministries of the congregation are faithful to that approach quickly become frustrated. Volunteer organizations like the church cannot be controlled. Members with a variety of life experiences bring different needs, assumptions, and skills to the congregation. God's grace surprises us. All four approaches to education may be present, at least to some degree. The educator asks, What differences do these approaches make? How do I guide a congregation into focusing on one or another of these approaches? Should I? How do I maintain my convictions and faith in the midst of these chaotic purposes? What am I to do?

These questions whirl through the educator's mind. We have already addressed the first question: What differences do these approaches make? We have seen that each approach begins at a different place and emphasizes different aspects of the process. All are efforts to live by Jesus' commandment to love God and love neighbor. However, because each approach relies on a different route to that goal, they appear very different in the programming of a congregation. Understanding and recognizing the strengths of each approach, observing the places where each is occurring in your congregation, and seeking to honor all four approaches can help to bridge the differences.

THE EDUCATOR AS GUIDE

The educator asks, How do I guide the congregation into focusing on one or another of these approaches? Should I?

The first step in guidance for the educator must be appreciating and observing what is already happening. Every congregation educates its people to love God and neighbor to some extent. We must learn to see how God's grace is already present, creating moments or glimpses of the world the way God intends for it to be.

We learn to see when we develop the skills of an ethnographer.[2] An ethnographer is one who studies the "ethnoi," the people. The methods employed by ethnographers recognize that humans are influenced by the other humans with whom they interact. Therefore, we can only begin to understand people by studying them in the midst of their lives, in the complexity of their relationships and motives. An effective congregational educator is one who looks and listens and seeks to understand the rich, thick tapestry of congregational life within which learning occurs and how it interacts with the life experiences of those who make up the congregation. The congregational educator must learn to see and hear the myriads of moments where congregational life is a context for the processes where people are making meaning.

What do we look and listen for? We look and listen for moments where hospitality happens, where the stranger is welcomed, where we are neighbors to one another, where we are filled with compassion and solidarity for those who suffer, where we share the gifts that God has given us generously with others, and where people are reflecting on the events of their lives in light of the Christian story and seeking to discern God's will for their lives. Bill's vulnerability when he said, "I was wondering about my mother. I need to believe that she is with God." was a moment of grace with the possibility of growth and transformation. Bill was asking for exploration of the meaning of both death and life with this question. Depending on how Michael answers the question, Bill could be reassured, cynical, hopeful, called into action toward the reign of God, or left in lethargic uncertainty. Michael listened, affirmed the genuine need of Bill's question, and responded as a neighbor who suffers with Bill, seeking to experience God's Word for himself as well as for Bill. Conversation about our lives in light of God's presence is religious education.

Educators also look for moments when conversation about our lives in light of God's presence might happen or should happen but does not. These opportunities are our agenda. When a Sunday school class such as Bill's is dodging the issues that are fermenting in the lives of its members, the educator can often find ways to stimulate or enable the conversations. Often, it is a matter of helping the participants to feel more safe. When the context for learning is hospitable and just, learners are freed to explore their stories and ask the questions that are a part of their meaning-making, a critical ingredient of effective contexts for learning.[3]

The key skill that Michael or Sally needs, as an educator, is listening. Congregational educators must learn to ask questions. More important, they must learn to be quiet and wait. The questions and needs will emerge. But they must emerge out of the life experience and spiritual journey of people like Bill. They must emerge out of the life experience and spiritual journey of the Sunday school class and its community. They must emerge out of the life events and communal identity of the congregation. This requires careful listening.

Often our impulse is to assume that *our* questions and needs are normative; we think, If I need to know this, then others do too. Certainly, human beings who are similar in age and status who live in the same community and belong to the same church will have great similarities. But the theological questions that arise out of our lives tend to be unique, shaped by our personalities, our culture, and the specific experiences of our lives—births and deaths, successes and failures, gains and losses.

We must also recognize that our ability to hear what Bill and others like him are asking or needing will always be limited by our own experiences and needs. No human being can ever entirely understand the needs or questions of another. Each of us is limited in what we can perceive. For instance, Michael hears the worry in Bill's questions about heaven. But Michael's mother is still alive. He could not know the intensity of the theological question Bill raised. He also did not know that Bill's mother had asked a cousin to sing "Precious Lord, Take My Hand" in her hospital room as she lay dying. Bill's question came out of his experience of his mother's tranquillity and assurance as she lay smiling and listening to that hymn. Bill knew his mother trusted in a welcome in heaven. He wanted confirmation that her trust was well founded.

How do educators look for these glimpses of God's transformative power within a congregation? We look with eyes of love. I believe that eyes of love are eyes that do not begin with judgment, but instead seek to see lives and groups as whole and complex, living within a web of forces. People do not come to a church in a vacuum; they come out of the totality of their lives. They bring the forces and experiences and needs of those lives to church. Educators must begin by taking seriously the whole of those lives. The issues of that reality should be a foundation of the curriculum for religious education. A pastor in a large city began his ministry with a door-to-door survey asking people why they did not go to church. They usually answered, "It's boring." Church is boring when it does not engage the real issues of our lives. It is boring when we must pretend to have our lives together—put on a happy face and our best clothes—even though we are worried about paying the credit card bill and about the arguments we have had with a loved one this week and the feeling of lethargy that has filled our days.

The Christian educator cannot see the glimpses of the reign of God that are already present in a congregation until he or she sees the people who are a part of the congregation in the complexity of the lives they lead, recognizing that each one seeks to be faithful, and that each one is a child of God touched by grace. Judgment is not the place to begin. Listening is. And the listening needs to occur with our shoes off, since we begin to know individual members of a congregation and the spiritual needs they bring to the congregation and we begin to realize that we are standing on holy ground. We must realize that this is the garden planted by God's grace.

In concrete terms, this means that a Christian educator must listen to each of those members of the Sunday school class with the assumption that he or she is speaking out of a life touched by grace. Each one has spiritual needs, shaped by all the experiences of her or his life. And the questions each one is asking are slightly different because of those unique experiences.

These skills of an ethnographer—to look, listen, and reflect on moments where God's grace is present—are the tools we use in seeking answers to the question, How do I guide the congregation into focusing on one or another of the approaches to Christian education? The ethnographic methods will help an educator to identify what approaches are already present and are a part of the life of the congregation. Identified and honored, they can be built upon and empowered. Unidentified, the educator is too often working at cross-purposes to the presuppositions and comforts of a congregation. The educator who persists in these cross-purposes will often end up unemployed and disillusioned. However, the educator who honors, utilizes, and encourages those practices of a congregation that are already present can build on and expand the repertoire of learning opportunities more easily and successfully.

THE RESEARCH PROCESS

How does an educator begin to understand the complex webs of interaction and meaning that are part of his or her congregation such as inviting, socializing, and teaching persons to love God and love neighbor? The assessment tool found in chapter 6 is a place to start. The educator can use this survey to identify the approach she or he most favors. As we educators uncover our own assumptions, we become more self-aware. We recognize that we act sometimes out of our own needs rather than the needs of others. What is most effective for our learning may not be most effective for the the learning of others. We begin by knowing ourselves.

In addition, an awareness of the approaches mapped by the four educational themes in this book and their goals, role of teacher and learner, processes for learning, contexts for learning, and implications for ministry [see chart, p. 21] can help the educator to understand the uncritical assumptions that inform the attitudes, needs, and dissatisfactions of people and groups within the congregation. For instance, the fictional conversation that begins this chapter between Bill and Michael reveals Michael's desire for a religious instruction approach. He wants to learn and understand. He expects learning to occur in a classroom setting. He needs the community of his Sunday school class to support him in the search. He wants a teacher to guide the process.

The recognition on Pastor Sally's part that important learning occurs when children stand alongside adults of all ages in the little sanctuary and sing the favorite hymns of that congregation is a recognition of the power of the faith community to educate. Those children may not be able to articulate what they have learned with words, but they experience in holistic ways what it means to be a part of the Body of Christ. Sally has sensitized herself to listen for and affirm these approaches to learning in her congregation. Once she sees that learning has progressed, she can look for ways to enrich or make more effective what is already happening.

Knowledge of the four approaches can help educators to recognize that important theological reflection occurs in many settings that are not labeled "education." For instance, at a women's spiritual retreat that provides a sabbath time apart for prayer and silence, some participants may find in their lives evidence of God's grace and leading. Other participants may experience the grace of acceptance around the dinner table that affirms their place in the family of God. These settings and many others can be opportunities to learn how to love God and neighbor.

Congregational educators can gain understanding of how learning is occurring by analyzing the curriculum content choices of classes and other groups. If a class uses the International Lesson Series, there is a curriculum plan published that details the scripture and the theological themes to be studied. Some classes choose books or topics they will study. These choices reveal much about the needs and interests of the group. Because the educator knows that a variety of needs, approaches, and lacks are a part of every group, she may find ways to enrich the curriculum content choices in her congregation.

The balance of worship, study, service, and fellowship in the life of a congregation is also a clue to its strengths and weaknesses. We learn to love God and neighbor through a combination of these activities. When they are out of balance, the learning will be incomplete. The educators in a congregation should always be sensitive to the balance of activities.

Charles R. Foster has coined the term, "event-centered education," to describe an approach to multifaceted learning that involves worship, study, service, and fellowship. Most Christian congregations in North America celebrate the events of Christmas and Easter. The preparations involve all generations over a period of time. Foster writes, "These seasonal events establish a structure for the interplay of a congregation's identification with certain paradigmatic events in our faith history and its responses over the years to local circumstances and relationships."[4] As we work together to decorate the sanctuary, to prepare the anthems, to study the scripture, to expand our prayer life around the seasons of Advent and Lent, we are preparing ourselves to celebrate the events of Christmas and Easter. We educate through the variety of activities for participation.

How does an educator begin to understand the complex webs of interaction and meaning that are part of his or her congregation? As we have discussed, we need to observe, ask questions, and listen in the midst of congregational life. The questions the educational ethnographer asks will be specific to each individual setting. Nevertheless, these questions will focus on persons and their lives, the dynamics of the congregation, and the environment of the community in which the people reside. In terms of persons, the goal of our questioning is to discern the issues that command the people's attention, how their faith affects the ways they engage these issues, and how their church assists or inhibits addressing these issues. In terms of the congregation, we seek to discern the places where the congregation honestly engages the issues of people's lives, where the congregation is particularly effective in helping people integrate faith and life, and how truth-telling and honest reflection can be enhanced.[5] In terms of the community, the educator needs to reflect on the forces that are affecting the lives of people; how culture, class, and values focus people's attention; and how the congregation can impact the forces that affect, and even define, the meanings with which people live.

RESEARCH LEADS TO EVALUATION AND REFLECTION

An educator who is effective has her antennae out at all times looking for moments where religious education is already happening or could be happening. However, this careful ethnography must go a step further: reflection and evaluation follows observation. The evaluation is critical if we are deciding on our next course of action. Some of what is happening in the congregation is effective and leads to deepening everyone's love of God and neighbor. Some of what is happening keeps people in bondage to old prejudices, guilt, and inertia. We clearly want to encourage the former and eliminate the latter. How do we determine which is which?

Three qualities are essential for Christian education that is effective and mutual: (1) the educator must see herself or himself as an **interpreter among interpreters;** (2) the contexts for learning must

create hospitable and just space; and (3) the congregation must **practice the presence of God.**[6]

An educator who seeks to reflect on and evaluate the contexts and opportunities for Christian education in a congregation must understand that she or he is an interpreter among interpreters: that is, a Christian educator must remember that "I, as the congregation educator, am not the only one with important insights and values. I am a participant along with the others in the congregation in this process of reflection and evaluation. The voices of all participants deserve to be heard. Thus, I (the educator) may not always know best. We listen to one another and honor the needs and desires of all." The practice of research, reflecting upon, and judging of the content and processes of congregational life must occur in the mutuality of interpreters together. An educator who is able to observe and recognize the four approaches outlined in this book has helpful information for evaluation. But this educator is still only one interpreter among a congregation of interpreters, many of whom will have important and helpful insights.

Those who are in the role of teacher will often be given power: power to define the learning goals, power to control the teaching and learning processes, power to control the range of ideas that are considered. In a congregation of interpreters, the people in the role of teacher seek to bring possibilities and resources to any question, but do not seek to control the outcome. Instead, the group is set free to explore interpretations and meanings together. In the class described by Bill at the beginning of this chapter, the person in the role of teacher needed to be sensitive to his questions. The teacher who understands that she or he is an interpreter among interpreters might bring a number of resources from the Bible and Christian tradition to the discussion. But the teacher/interpreter would not try to enforce only one possible interpretation. To be a colearner, a teacher must listen carefully to the questions and answers of all participants, helping each to offer "answers" in an atmosphere of shared vulnerability and mutual search for truth.[7]

When the interpreters who are evaluating and planning for education discover contexts within the life of the congregation where mutuality is not occurring, interventions may be necessary. For instance, teachers who belittle or disregard the contributions of learners are denying the mutuality that is critical for learning, which can shape or transform our relationship to the God of grace. These teachers must learn to relate in more mutual ways or be replaced.

Listening and shared vulnerability is the starting point for hospitable and just space. In order for participants in a congregation to have the greatest possible opportunities for growth, they must be able to bring the questions, celebrations, and griefs of their lives to contexts for theological reflection that are hospitable and just. A hospitable context is one in which the individual feels the security of "home." One feels welcomed.

However, hospitable and just space is not just a matter of a "warm, fuzzy" atmosphere. It is dependent upon both seeking relationships and honoring differences. To hold ourselves in relationship and yet to honor difference is difficult at times, yet it promotes growth. When we have to define the ground on which we stand against the ground upon which another stands, we clarify. And when we do not allow ourselves to dismiss, demonize, or ignore the "other," we look with more depth and dimension on where we stand. When we honor all parts of the ecosystem, we risk differences of opinion that often cannot be integrated or synthesized. The dissonance and the ambiguity they cause may be painful. Yet we need to learn to live in their midst if we are to incarnate mutuality and build a just learning community.[8]

Brother Lawrence's notion that the route to faithfulness is to practice the presence of God has caught the imagination of many Christians because it is so simple and yet so profound. Practicing the presence of God is the final criterion for evaluating the contexts for learning in a congregation. When we practice God's presence, we seek to live in "an habitual, silent and secret conversation of the soul with God."[9] When all learning in the congregation includes this dimension, we look for God's leading but also allow for God's surprises. We risk entering into relationship with one another knowing that we are in relationship with God also. We "pay attention" to one another even as we "pay attention" to God. Practicing presence also raises our awareness of how God's graceful presence undergirds our learning. We are able to let go of our defensiveness and resistance and explore meanings in light of God's grace.

Another dimension of practicing the presence of God is honoring the whole of the Christian tradition. Interpreters will be limited by the fund of religious images, stories, and concepts available to them. For instance, if they do not know the parable of the loving father and his two sons (Luke 15:11-32), they know little of forgiveness and grace. If they do not know the parable of the good Samaritan (Luke 10:25-37), they cannot understand the concept of neighbor. Lacking the stories of creation found in Genesis, they might not appreciate the richness and goodness of all creation; they might not recognize our responsibility for stewardship of that creation; they could not begin to understand the God-given sabbath. A rich and diverse fund of images, stories, and concepts from our religious tradition can prompt faith questions as well as guide us. This means that the interpreter must be steeped in her or his faith tradition. But it also means that the educator must attempt to provide opportunities for everyone in the congregation to acquire a rich fund from the religious tradition.

In practicing the presence of God we ask, What is God's call to us in this situation? We seek answers in the Bible, in the Christian tradition, in our own experiences and in those of our fellow interpreters, and through the gift of reason. Through it all, we listen for God's answers. God empowers us with moments when we live justly and lovingly. Those moments provide hope and possibilities. We seek to join with God in working toward the reign of God.

THE CONGREGATIONAL EDUCATOR'S IDENTITY AND VOCATION

The questions remaining for the educator to ask are, "How do I maintain my convictions and faith in the midst of these chaotic congregational purposes?" and "What am I to do?" We have seen that all four approaches explored in this book are probably present, sometimes competing and sometimes complementing one another. We have seen that moments of grace and evidence of the present character of the reign of God abound. Yet, the educator will also find times when the personhood of children, youth, and adults is violated; times when the opportunities for confronting profound theological questions are lost; times when the life of the congregation fails to call people to greater faithfulness and discipleship; and times when bigotry and prejudice reign in the midst of congregational life.

I believe the only way to survive this complexity and sinfulness is to walk with integrity, seeking to embody the principles we use for evaluation. Thus we understand that each of us is considered "an interpreter among interpreters." We do not claim more authority than that. We listen and know that we can always learn from others. In addition, we seek to create safe and hospitable contexts for learning. And we practice the presence of God, continuing to study and reform the Christian tradition, seeking truth and justice as we open ourselves to the gifts of God's grace.

In the opening chapter of this book, Jack Seymour described the context for Christian education: "In a world of fear and anxiety, we must find ways of acknowledging the lives of people."[10] The angel said to Mary and then to the shepherds, "Fear not." Jesus told his followers, "Do not worry." Yet life is full of fear and worry along with joy and hope. When congregational life provides opportunities to confront, heal, or celebrate those feelings in a hospitable and just space in a setting rich with the resources of the Christian tradition, it offers meaningful and effective Christian education.

8
Agenda for the Future

JACK L. SEYMOUR and
___ DONALD E. MILLER___

In our time God's Word calls forth new communities and hopes while sustaining continuity with God's past revelations. Believers, individually and together, experience God's Word as saving grace, as a community-forming presence, as a beacon toward the future. The Word is radically shaped by the historical context into which it comes. Today in our world God's Word comes as a healing and empowering presence among historical tendencies moving toward fragmentation and alienation. We must declare, as has the Church of the Brethren, that we are "continuing the work of Jesus. Peacefully. Simply. Together."[1]

History is full of dramatic changes and biblical faith was born in such times. The church is both a source and result of such changes. The church stands for both continuity and new possibilities. These seemingly contradictory roles of faith have often led to conflict and dissension among the faithful. The special challenge of Christian education is to move beyond such contradictions.

In the nineteenth century, the Union Sunday School movement spread into regions west of the Alleghenies that were being settled. The idea of a Sunday school in every locale addressed the need for community formation throughout the Midwest and later the West. After the Civil War, Sunday school leaders challenged the church to care for new immigrants, to reform child labor laws, and to seek justice for those who lived in city tenements. Furthermore, the influence of the International Lesson Series addressed a widening global concern. Such a global concern had always been present in Roman Catholicism, which was itself struggling to understand how to adapt faith to the new context of U.S. democracy and religious multiplicity. Catholic educators believed that

110

through parochial schools they could give their youth a religious vision for participating in American democracy. Furthermore, changes in Christian religious education in the twentieth century have been focused on how to help people hold on to the faith and encounter the world with new life.[2]

Again we are at a point of radical change in the life of the church and in the developments of global culture. As the longtime Sunday school teacher, Frank Donnell, who was described in chapter 1 asked: "Somehow we have not made it possible or easy for people to be theological in their everyday relationships and conversations. . . . And, yet, it's the dominant element in so many of our lives. . . . Why aren't we able to communicate faith?"[3] As we explore the questions from our lives that overwhelm us, we hope for experiences of joy and grace and we search for meaning for our lives.

We are confronted with a perplexing and ever-changing world. We ask, What does faithfulness mean? How can we participate with God and others in experiencing hope, grace, and justice? As we have seen throughout these chapters, education in faith is rooted in a community of memory where stories, beliefs, and practices must be taught. Education is located in communities of people in congregations, synagogues, and assemblies of faith that are seeking to support one another, teach their faiths, and explore new meanings for new realities. Then, too, education is connected to our personal journeys of grace and pain where we want to live with hope and vitality as we join with others in the healing of creation.

After conversing about meanings, beliefs, and practices in a confusing world, Frank Donnell further commented, "What struck me is how much searching there is, and—interestingly—not too many discoveries. . . . Everybody's sure that there's something [meaning and grace] valuable out there." He was puzzled about the lack of "discoveries, insights, or revelations." He asked, Do we not recognize the revelations that are present, are there none, or do we just settle for old patterns and not see God's new action in our midst? How are we to respond to his struggle? How do we educate to recognize God's new actions breaking through old patterns? How do we find the endurance to keep seeking God's will in the midst of the pain and struggle of our lives, our failures, betrayals, gifts, and love in a chaotic world whose anguish and hatred seem so intractable? How do we make it possible "to be theological" in our everyday relationships?

THE SOCIAL SITUATION FACING THE CHURCH

The context for congregational and denominational life is the deep flux of a given historical time. Christian education is rooted in experienced, historical participation. So the agenda for the future must consider the social challenges that are shaping the close of the twentieth century and the beginning of the twenty-first.

1. The new technologies for transportation and electronic communication are transforming life around the globe. Faster trains and planes carry people to almost any part of the earth in a matter of hours. Television, cellular phones, faxes, and electronic mail bring people from every part of the world in touch with one another in a matter of seconds. People are confronted with global events in vivid, memorable images.

These new modes of transportation and communication are arresting, absorbing, even addictive. The majority of people, including children, spend many hours a day watching television. Some people spend endless hours surfing the world using the Internet. The computer and the fax machine have become necessities for business, often replacing employees. The television is a shaper of moral values.

2. A change that seems to accompany the new technologies is increasing individualism. Television, for example, is a very passive medium through which a viewer is spoon-fed with dramatic and motivating images. Stories are not informed by the needs of local communities so much as by what will catch the attention of an ever larger number of viewers. Violence, sexual images, and moral transgressions are great attention getters. We experience television in our isolated individualism; we do not need to watch it in community.

Furthermore, the trend in new housing is to erect developments that are not connected to the history of the locality. These housing developments are sometimes fenced and occasionally guarded, all of which heighten the separation from the local history. Old English marketing names are often chosen because they sell—names like Canterbury Hills or Wellington Manor. Thereby the local historical lore is obscured or forgotten. Many of the residents of these developments then travel to wholly different communities to work.

The effects of both television and housing result in the erosion of local community loyalty. People are isolated. Alexis de Tocqueville, a French commentator on early U.S. life, suggested that the distinctive quality of life in the United States is the degree to which people organize locally to address their community problems.[4] In this new individualism, U.S. citizens seem to be losing interest in voluntary associations. Whether bowling leagues, fraternal lodges, school PTAs, or the church, participation is down. The roots of community life and of democratic interaction are weakened.

3. A third historical trend for the U.S. is the coming together of many cultures. In part, the coincidence of cultures comes from television news, where one can experience the life and practices of people from around the world. The world of the Internet can have a similar effect upon computer users. Images from Somalia, Haiti, and Bosnia live in the memories of most people. Millions of people across the earth simultaneously watch Michael Jordan play basketball. Foods from many cultures (i.e., tacos, egg rolls, salsa) are displayed for viewers everyday.

Cultural interaction is also the result of the population movements across the world. For example, like the Europeans did a century ago, persons from Latin American and Asian nations are moving into the United States. Poverty, war, and oppression are frequently motives for their relocation, as is the seductive power of American culture transported throughout the world by business and media.

Encountering persons from different cultures with different traditions and values stretches traditional patterns of interaction. Islam, for example, is the fastest growing religion in the United States. Most Europeans who emigrated to the U.S. "melted" into the great melting pot with seemingly shared common values. Cultural values were preserved in private parts of people's lives, such as holidays and home celebrations. Of course, not all groups melted together. The culture pushed to its margins those who did not seem to fit, like African Americans who had been stolen from their lands and traditions. Moreover, many of the distinctive gifts of cultural groups were ignored and cultural traditions violated.

We have reached a time when the diversity of peoples needs to be addressed. We need to learn to build a world together, but we are not clear how this process occurs with so many different values and traditions. Therefore, cultural interaction has been accompanied by culture wars, deep disputes about different cultural values. The struggles over sexual values, abortion, ordination of women, religion in the public schools, and global mission are intense in both the church and the wider communities. The extreme of cultural conflict is to be found among those who want ethnic cleansing, as is the case in Bosnia, where Roman Catholic, Orthodox, and Muslim values are pitted against one another.

4. A fourth characteristic of our time is an increasing separation of rich and poor. The striking difference between the First and Third World countries, the haves and the have-nots, is a characteristic of the twentieth century. For example, the economic reforms in the former Soviet Union have been accompanied by a stark separation of the newly rich from the many poor.

In the United States the increasing wealth of some is accompanied by increasing numbers of both rural and urban poor. Even the middle class seems under siege. Large companies are downsizing by dismissing workers. The result is that many middle management people feel threatened.

The economic situation has created ghettos of despair and hopelessness where an underground economy flourishes and violence results. Churches cannot ignore this situation because of the biblical injunction for justice. Drive-by shootings occur even on church steps, sometimes involving members of a congregation. Violence resulting from hopelessness is a primary social problem.

5. A fifth characteristic is that of an aging society. Many people are living longer, largely because of medical and nutritional advances. The aging population is seen in the graying of the

church. Middle-aged persons are often caring not only for children, and sometimes grandchildren, but also for aging parents.

Developed countries like the United States have fewer children than developing countries. But far more ominous is the fact that societies have become unfriendly to children in both developed and developing countries. Television has played its part by feeding children a plethora of adult images, often with little moral guidance. Young children often face violence, drugs, and harassment that children of an earlier generation did not experience. Public education seems to be eroding. Many students of parents with financial resources retreat to private school havens, leaving public schools with tremendous needs and few resources.

THE DECLINING VITALITY OF THE CONGREGATION

Congregations reside within the trends just described. The result is often a declining vitality within the congregation. Some megachurches have been able to attract thousands of worshipers by using drama, small groups, contemporary media, and popular music. Other congregations feel that such actions are concessions to popular culture. The structures used by congregations in the future is critical because the congregation is the primary setting for formal Christian education. The church is one agency among many others in our culture offering meaning and values.

Congregations once were local representatives for denominational values. In past decades, people knew what it meant to be Lutheran, Presbyterian, Brethren, Methodist, or Catholic. Each church could be trusted to use denominational curriculum and to teach the values born in the conflicts that formed the different denominations. Uniformly this is not the case any longer as denominational curriculum sales plummet and each local group of people reflects its own unique identity. The people in most congregations are a mixture of denominational backgrounds. In many cases denominational loyalty is not as significant as it once was.

Each of these trends affects congregations and denominations.

1. The new transportation allows people to travel much greater

distances to a congregation. The result is that as people move, more congregations are regional rather than community based. Regional congregations may lose their connections with the particular neighborhood in which they are located. For example, some wealthy congregations located in the center of cities often become an anachronism drawing people from suburbs and providing expansive programs while ignoring homelessness at their steps and business decisions made across the street.

Television could give people a greater sense of the world's needs and thereby a wider sense of mission. The more predominant effect seems to be giving people a higher expectation of being entertained. The quick pace, high energy, vivid image, pop music, sound bite, and moral relativism of television erodes reflective, meditative, morally committed spirituality of traditional Christianity. So the congregation is caught in a dilemma of how to reach and hold people.

2. The trends that erode commitment to local communities, and participation in voluntary associations, also result in lessening church attendance for many congregations. People who are not connected with the community, whose business community is elsewhere, who do not want to be absorbed in the busyness of congregational life, who find television and computers more satisfying than a church council meeting or worship services, are dropouts from church life. Today, people do not need the church to fill their time or to provide associations as they once did on the lonely frontiers. This loss of church participation parallels the loss of participation in other local community activities, and bodes poorly for the nourishment of a democratic society.

Foundation executive Craig Dykstra has connected this individualism of society to the church. People seek an "expressive spirituality" where each person decides for oneself what religious experience one wants. The social researcher Robert Wuthnow further describes this religious individualism, "Our faith is no longer something we inherit, but something for which we shop. It provides us with security, not by protecting us with a high wall, but by giving us resources, by plugging us into the right networks, and by giving us the confidence to bargain for what we need."[5]

The focus on individualism and the decline in participation fur-

116

ther depletes the energy that congregations have to understand and address the wider global world. The complexity and chaos of the world seems intractable and too often people withdraw behind walls of comfort, only sharing with and supporting others like themselves in hope of holding back the fear of the future. The way that we learn to address these global issues is crucial. The church has historically participated in the forming of communities. Its experience and values are needed in the mix of decision making for the future.

3. The encounter of cultural difference results in a threat to congregational vitality. Often the culture wars over sexuality, abortion, ordination of women, religion in the schools, and global mission divide congregations. Sometimes they split the congregation from the denomination. This occurrence is not new to the church, as a similar situation can be seen in the debates about slavery in an earlier era.

Because of the threat of division, people feel uncomfortable. Many are not at ease speaking about their views or about their own intensely personal experience, because someone else in the congregation will be offended. Also they may feel that their views will not be accepted and they will be judged. When one cannot speak about one's own intensely personal experience, one cannot speak about one's faith in its fullness. The result weakens the vitality of the congregation. The touchiness of issues affects the whole congregation from children's programs to adult mission projects.

We live in a world of multiple faiths and religious movements. We have resources in our traditions to encounter one another, to listen, and to pray to the God of life and creation. Yet, the task looks too great; the pain is immense. Fear overwhelms. Only with hope can we address our differences and seek a world together. Theological reflection and interreligious dialogue are critical to hope.

4. The separation of the rich and the poor, along with accompanying violence resulting from this division, is a context congregations too often ignore. Congregations have historically stratified by class. However the gospel is predisposed toward the poor and the vulnerable. The church that does not work at these disparities is not being faithful.

In the same way, the Bible is predisposed toward nonviolence. Jesus Christ came as the Prince of Peace, which means that every Christian congregation has a primary calling to be a peacemaker. The increasing violence in this country strikes at the vitality of the gospel.

5. The aging of society has led to many aging congregations. When these congregations are unable to attract younger families, they may only look forward to their own demise. If the congregation is an unfriendly place for children, a pale reflection of the wider community, then it cannot expect to attract younger families.

Congregations are vital places when values are reformed and passed from one generation to another as people confront life together. We need to simultaneously ask about how a congregation supports those older persons who have given their lives to form the congregation and how the congregation continues to teach the faith to the new generation. The way in which we address issues of the future is rooted in the way that we interact as generations within congregations and the wider society.

CONGREGATIONAL EDUCATION

Christian education is at its best as it assists persons in dealing with the crucial issues of personal and social life in light of the gospel. Christian education teaches the faith tradition first recorded in the Bible, so that people take on the identity of Jesus and gather resources to seek God's will in day-by-day encounters. Theological reflection occurs for each individual believer as he or she confronts and makes decisions about how to live faithfully in the moments of daily life. Christian education must provide open spaces where people can learn the faith tradition, engage that tradition with issues of life, and seek to live together in ways that are faithful to God.

The prayer that Jesus taught captures for Christians the task. As we pray "give us this day our daily bread," we cry out for the very food to sustain our lives. Furthermore, we cry out for God's love and support and for the love and support of our spiritual friends as we walk into a world of seemingly intractable problems and personal insecurities. Daily bread is everything that we need to sustain life. "Give us this day our daily bread" is a cry for life. In addition, the focus of the prayer is "Your kingdom come. Your will be done." We believe that God is present in the world luring us into actions of hope, wholeness, and justice. We believe that we are to be God's partners, yet we know that our will often misleads and we are broken on the commitments, events, and relationships of life. We pray at our depths, "O God, lead us into your will." Christian education is a setting of conversation where we seek to encounter the questions of daily bread, where we learn to forgive, seek deliverance from evil, and pray that we can live into God's reign of wholeness, meaning, hope, and justice for the world.

The causes of declining church membership are complex. We may not have adequately invited people into the experiences of vitality and grace at the center of religious faith. We have been too tentative in claiming the gifts we have encountered from a living God. We have been too tentative in calling people to journey together to address life's pain with hope and grace.

But the decline in mainstream churches does not seem to have primarily resulted from this lack of invitation. New members have come; new commitments have been made. Rather, the loss of members has resulted from those who have fallen away from participation. Children drop away after membership classes and many mainstream churches have cleared their rolls of those who no longer attend. The loss of membership is a loss of those who had once joined and participated in the church.

What does this mean? Some congregations have not adequately helped people engage the faith as it speaks to life. Again as Frank Donnell noted, "Everybody's sure that there's something [meaning and grace] valuable out there," yet, there is a lack of "discoveries, insights, or revelations." Why?

A look at vital congregations shows people who want to listen, celebrate, reflect, and mourn what is in their lives (brokenness, violence, addiction, loss of love, poverty, oppression, alienation, transitions, injustices, the community on their doorsteps). They want to make the gospel live as a promise that empowers the

119

struggle. People cry out to God from their need. Theological reflection is born in the heartfelt struggle of people making sense of these experiences. People pray for hope, meaning, and God's guidance.

Vital congregations may not "give" answers. In fact, too easy answers close the conversation. However, what is present is a vitality that searches to answer Frank Donnell's question: Are there no "discoveries, insights, or revelations"? Are we just not recognizing them? Does settling for old patterns block us from seeing God's new actions? A mark of vital congregations is engaging the immediate problems of self, life, world, family circumstance, and intransigent community problems together with a sense of support and hope in a God who can answer prayer, give daily bread, and teach us to forgive as we seek God's reign.

While the problems of the world we address are complex and immense, we must address them through coalitions of people who are often very different from ourselves. We need to know ourselves and know how to be involved in cross-cultural dialogue; both are issues for Christian education. We need to know how to build coalitions of care and justice that respond step-by-step to the vulnerable. Education empowers us to move from conversation to faithful living. We live "daily bread" as we reach out to those in our lives in our wholeness, with love and hope, knowing that these acts of love are set in a wider context of the world. Christian education fosters a movement theologically informed by the witnesses from the past to address the crucial personal and social issues of our day with faithful current analysis and a vision that is informed by the long-term history of God emerging in a people. Christian education provides open spaces to practice God's presence and to share our lives and vulnerabilities in hospitality and love. Vital congregations engage the faith as it speaks to life!

MAPPING CHRISTIAN EDUCATION

As we see through the chapters of this book, Christian educators are seeking to address the cries of the culture, the integrity of theological traditions, and the experiences of people. Christian educator Sara Little has argued, "There is no one clue, no dominant theory" for Christian education today.[6] That is precisely what we see in the chapters of this book. There is no one clue, yet there appears to be an emerging consensus about the tasks of Christian education in this day of cultural diversity and profound social change. Four clues coalesce in these chapters: (1) *facing into the world is the task of Christian education;* (2) *the congregation is the primary setting for Christian education;* (3) *theological reflection is the methodology,* and (4) *religious learning occurs in hospitable, just, and open spaces for conversation and truth-telling.*

Little has argued that "education is recognized as a field requiring interdisciplinary collaboration. It is public. It is diverse. It is dependent on a living religion for vitality."[7] These chapters evidence educators drawing on a wealth of resources of interdisciplinary collaboration from theology to social analysis, from developmental theory to research on community life, from educational research to analysis of the ways that humans make meaning. Moreover, Christian education is dependent on a "living religion" emerging in the lives of people as they seek both individually and together to understand their calls from God to live faithfully in the midst of the world. The resources of a "living religion" are experiences out of which settings and processes of Christian education are formed: from theological traditions to processes of theological reflection, from practices of worship and prayer to coalitions acting for justice in the world, from community support in times of crisis and life transitions to daily decisions informed by discernment.

Facing into the world is the task of Christian education. Through Christian education we face into the world, explore the deepest meanings of our lives, engage one another, and partner with a God seeking wholeness and meaning for all life. Facing into the world includes social analysis as people look at the forces that shape their lives and seek to understand the context within which they live and breathe. We must take seriously the issues and problems that are both at the edge of consciousness and those that are staring us in the face. Hope to engage a world that seems to be falling apart cannot be accomplished if we deny the brokenness of the world or if we run away in despair. Hope arises as we face into the world.

Yet, we do not face into the world alone; we do it in community. We recognize the gifts that we have for addressing the world's pain and brokenness. Human associations like Habit for Humanity, the Carter Center,[8] shelters for the abused, AIDS hostels, and churches provide us with colleagues who lead the way. The arts, science, and our knowledge of how to build coalitions for the common good are means we can use in our common response to the world.

Furthermore, facing into the world begins as we listen to the people of God in local churches and communities express the meanings and issues at the center of their lives. Robert Coles, in an interview about his book *The Call of Service,* spoke about the power he saw in the lives of people he interviewed. This power is present in our congregations of faith as people speak from their hearts, as people share the deepest concerns and needs for belonging, care, meaning, and guidance.

Listening to people demonstrated to Coles both the pain encountered in life and the resources of hope addressing it. "I am a witness. . . . The people I write about are themselves witnesses who possess a moral passion that I have needed, and that has been very important in my personal life. . . . There is in the lives of the people I write about a kind of honor and decency that professionals like me ought to salute and try to learn from."[9]

Facing into the world means entering into the lives of the people with whom we work, live, and worship as well as others who are different from ourselves and who we may encounter as strangers. Our vocations in life are found as we struggle to be faithful. Hope is possible only as we honestly face the pain and discover colleagues standing beside us, moral passion, the grace that cuts away denial, and the grace that offers new life. This tension of hope and of honestly facing pain are also evident in the persons about whom Coles has written, those called to service:

Each person is a mix of hope and discouragement. We all struggle with the hopeful side of life and the downside of life—perhaps at the same time. Service does present many people with a real opportunity for discouragement, and I used the word "opportunity" advisedly. At times service brings people to an awareness of some of the rock-bottom horrors and injustices of life. Such experiences can help people come to terms with life's meaning because suffering can be related to a transfiguration of sorts—a transfiguration of suffering. Through service one is exposed to suffering, and it gives one pause. . . . I don't know how grace comes, but I don't think it's just handed out to people who are smiling all the time and go to church every Sunday.[10]

Hope is born in engaging life truthfully. Hope and grace do not come in the wish or the desire; they arise out of the action.

The congregation is the primary setting for Christian education. Meaning occurs within the personal reflection of each person. Meaning cannot be given or granted by another. We each accept meanings out of which we will live. Of course, through the ordinary times of life, we tend to accept the older meanings that have been formed in the crucibles of our lives. We take things for granted. A meal cooked by another for us means love instead of obligation. Going to work means that we have a vocation rather than we are stressed to our limits by fear and confusion.

Many of life's meanings come through the communities of identity and memory in which we were formed and through which we learned the purposes of life. Small-town life, for example, has a code of behavior and interpretations of life that are taught in the stories people share and in the practices by which they interact. This is equally true in other communities. Children who grow up on the "wrong side of town" soon learn that they have been given an identity. People who participate deeply in the life of a congregation soon learn that their associations profoundly influence what they believe. The practices we encounter on our jobs focus our lives. The patterns of family life shape the ways we think about ourselves. People seeking freedom from addictions band together with others of like experiences to share the happenings of their lives, to reenforce new meanings, and to support one another on the hard journeys of freedom.

At times of crisis, when the accepted meanings provided by our communities of memory are challenged or shattered, we either remake meanings out of the resources of our lives or we have to transform our lives as we discover new meanings by which our lives are guided. The crises of life—death, loss of a job or accepting a new job, a broken relationship—and the injustice and oppression we encounter as groups try to enforce their life patterns on our lives calls us to remake meanings or to transform our lives by new meanings.[11]

Of course, life calls us to theological reflection; life calls each of us in unique ways because we are all different. Ultimately we each are alone to believe, explore, and interpret our lives. We each believe for ourselves; yet we are influenced by the meanings our culture shares with us, media portrayals, and life experiences.

The wider culture clearly influences the ways we think about religious faith. Media portrayals and news sensationalism influence the way we feel about religious people. An example is the atrocious ways that the U.S. media has treated Islam. A historic and great moral faith has been portrayed as an equivalent to piracy. Muslims in the U.S. have a right to be outraged by the way the media has defined them. Their faithfulness, deep commitment to God, moral living, and community responsibility have been ignored.

Communities affect us. If we are to gain the repertoire of Christian faith from which we can draw to explore life meanings, we need to encounter these images, stories, symbols, beliefs, and practices through participation in a community of memory and identity, a congregation. In congregations, we explore patterns of reflection, we consider faith values, and we reflect on our lives, vocations, and discipleship.[12] The community of faith provides resources for faith reflection by inviting us into a repertoire of meanings. The community of faith provides settings to practice meaning-making. The community of faith provides support in times of life crisis and transition as we interpret our lives in light of faith. The community of faith also provides powerful experiences that touch us with the depth of life. In spite of the social trends eroding congregational life and the lack of effectiveness of many congregations, congregations are still the primary locus for learning Christian traditions, values, and practices. Congregations are the primary places where people can reflect on their lives in light of the Christian faith.

Theological reflection is the methodology. Speaking about groups of Christians around the world who seek to be faithful, theologians Samuel Amirtham and John S. Pobee write

Ministry belongs to the whole people of God. Therefore, all God's people need to be appropriately equipped for ministry. . . . People are not only eager to learn theology; they are also creating theology. . . . Christians who have never had access to formal theology are learning afresh to relate faith to life, worship to work, prayer to action, proclamation to protest, in new creative ways. They discover in that process that they are doing theology, and that they need theology in their search for new forms of Christian obedience. . . . People need theology and, more particularly, theology needs people.[13]

Relating faith to life, worship to work, prayer to action, proclamation to protest is the work of theology and education. Theological reflection occurs as we encounter God's Word addressing us in our lives in the world.

The essays in this book point to theological reflection grounded in people's lives as the method of Christian education. The theological tradition is dynamic. The people of God are doing theology when they seek to discern God's will for their lives, when God's address becomes a personal commitment. Christian education needs to provide opportunities for people to learn the resources of Christian faith. Moreover, Christian education needs to assist people to explore the natural processes by which they make meaning and decide to act in the daily moments of life. Therefore Christian education is both learning the resources of the Christian tradition and practicing using those resources for meaning-making.

In her book, *Encountering God,* Diana Eck, a professor of comparative religion, has used the image of a river to describe religious faith. "Religious traditions are far more like rivers than stones."[14] Religious traditions are not solid objects against which we submit our lives. Rather they are flowing, lively rivers into which we enter. Our reflections, our experiences contribute to the meanings and practices of the faith. She further writes, "Like the Ganges or the Gallatin, they are flowing and changing. Sometimes they dry up in arid land; sometimes they radically change course and move out to water new territory. All of us contribute to the river of our traditions. We do not know how we will change the river or be changed as we experience its currents."[15]

We are engaging in theology as we explore the deepest issues of our lives in light of God, in light of our theological traditions that witness to God's presence in the world. Eck further adds, "Theological questions are not merely theoretical; they are the life and death questions of real people attempting to live with intellectual and personal honesty in a world too complex for simplistic answers."[16] When we search for what we want most deeply, it coincides with what God wants for us.

The community of faith is a setting for people to learn the resources of Christian faith and to practice exploring and discerning the meanings that define one's identity and focus one's vocation. These processes of exploring and discerning are the processes of theological reflection. Thomas Jarrell, a journalist, talked about his journey as a Christian person.

I think we all, at least all human beings I've ever met, have a need to work out their connection with the universe, birth and death and . . . suffering. With their fellow human beings. And that's a language that is traditionally the language of sacred texts—where it's theology talking about beginnings and endings, and there's dealing with suffering, and with the primal milestones in human life.[17]

These issues of transition and the meanings we ordinarily encounter in everyday life are the cries out of which we come to God in prayer, theological reflection, and commitment.

Religious learning occurs in hospitable, just, and open spaces for conversation and truth-telling. The issues of our lives make us vulnerable. The meanings on which we have staked our lives are often broken open and we are, in turn, broken open. These deepest concerns, as well as the questions that most trouble us, need to be shared in hospitable and just spaces where our vulnerabilities can be respected.

Too often because of fear, or even care, congregations close off the discussion of people's lives. People are blocked from telling their truths, their questions, and their pain. The church runs away from issues of sexuality, of conflict, of addiction, and of passions that are heartfelt. Without the freedom to tell, people cannot connect their lives to the faith.

Thomas Jarrell continued his reflection on the church. "There are lots of people exploring and faithfully attempting to keep the faith . . . translating the meaning of religious experience into languages consistent with the everyday." He pleads that the church provide a safe and open space for this translation.[18]

Another layperson, Mary Bracken, an engineer, commented that she left the church at one point because the church denied major parts of her life experience. "Those are the kinds of things that caused me to leave the church for many years. Because it could not accept my sexuality, everything that was a part of me. If you can't accept that, then I'm having a problem." She further described the church: "The fundamental opportunity of the church is to make a safe place, not as scary as it is. Homo sapiens are hurt animals, and they need to come together somewhere. They need these safe harbors."[19]

Safe harbors are needed for people to open the depth of their lives and ask, Where is God? Who does God want me to be? How can I be faithful to God? How can I be whole? Of course, not every place in a church will be safe and open. We need to provide multiple opportunities where groups can grow together, where colleagues are free to mentor and care, and where people can share in truth and honestly heartfelt concerns.

Providing multiple opportunities takes planning and attention. Not every group will be hospitable at every moment. Groups need time to form. Groups need openness to tell the truth. Groups need methods and procedures that invite people to connect faith and life. Groups need supportive structures that give them priority in congregational life and keep them from becoming too narrow in interest. The Holy Spirit draws us through these consistent structures to moments where we can speak the truth and address the everyday life issues people bring.

Christian education is a theological conversation among persons who are facing into the world. As we approach the twenty-first century, we ask: How do we explore life experiences with meanings of the faith? How do we consider the wealth of information and values at our disposal? How do we discern how to live as Christians in a world of rapid change, increasing diversity, ethnic violence, enhanced networks of communication, limited resources, improved technologies of health, and mounting gaps of wealth and opportunity? How do we recognize God's guidance and how do we transcend old patterns to respond to what God is doing new in our midst?

The answer is that Christian education provides a context in which people engage life with the great traditions of faith, religious experiences, and the resources of our cultures. We seek to know what our lives mean in light of God and how we are called to participate in God's grace, love, and hope in the midst of life. This is the journey that we engage together. We invite you to participate in this journey.

As you educate, add your map to the terrain of faith. Pray "thy will be done." Commit your life. Continue the work of Jesus toward meaning, wholeness, and justice.

NOTES

ACKNOWLEDGMENTS

1. Sara Little, "The 'Clue' to Religious Education," *Union Seminary Quarterly Review* 47 (1993): 20.

2. Ibid.

CHAPTER 1. APPROACHES TO CHRISTIAN EDUCATION

1. The stories in the introduction are from research Margaret Ann Crain and I have been conducting on lay theology. See "The Cry for Theology I: Laity Speak About Theology," *P.A.C.E.: Professional Approaches for Christian Educators* (February 1996), 29-34; "The Cry for Theology II: Laity Speak About the Church," *P.A.C.E.: Professional Approaches for Christian Educators* (March 1996), 43-46; "Thrashing in the Night: Laity Speak About Religious Knowing," *Religious Education* (spring 1997).

2. For further reading on these topics, see *Educating Christians,* by Jack L. Seymour, Margaret Ann Crain, and Joseph V. Crockett (Nashville: Abingdon Press, 1993), 150-58.

3. Jack L. Seymour and Donald E. Miller, eds., *Contemporary Approaches to Christian Education* (Nashville: Abingdon Press, 1982).

4. John Westeroff, *Will Our Children Have Faith?* (San Francisco: HarperSanFrancisco, 1984); Berard Marthaler, "Socialization as a Model for Catechesis," in *Foundations of Religious Education,* ed. Padraic O'Hare (New York: Paulist Press, 1978), 64-72; Charles R. Foster, *Teaching in the Community of Faith* (Nashville: Abingdon Press, 1982); James Fowler, *Stages of Faith* (New York: Harper & Row, 1981); Mary Wilcox, *Developmental Journey* (Nashville: Abingdon Press, 1979); Sara Little, *To Set One's Heart: Belief and Teaching in the Church* (Atlanta: John Knox Press, 1983); James Michael Lee, *The Flow of Religious Instruction: A Social Science Approach* (Mishawaka, Ind.: Religious Education Press, 1973).

5. Robert Bezilla, *Religion: Past, Present and Future in the United States and Canada* (Princeton, N.J.: Princeton Religious Research Center, 1995).

6. Stephen Carter, *The Culture of Disbelief* (New York: Basic Books, 1993).

7. See Hans Kuhn, "An Initial Declaration Towards a Global Ethic," (paper presented at the 1993 Parliament of the World's Religions, Chicago, Ill., August 28–September 5, 1993). Also see Gerald O. Barney, *Global 2000 Revisited: What Shall We Do?* (Arlington, Va.: The Millennium Institute, 1993).

8. Douglas John Hall, *Thinking the Faith* (Minneapolis: Fortress Press, 1991).

9. Wilfred Cantwell Smith, *Towards a World Theology* (Philadelphia: Westminster Press, 1981), 26.

10. Ibid., 29.

CHAPTER 2. EDUCATING FOR SOCIAL TRANSFORMATION

1. In the Gospel According to Matthew, the Beatitudes are the introduction of the Sermon on the Mount. Curriculum of the reign of God would be actually a more fitting name for the material found in chapters 5–7, given Matthew's didactic orientation and Jesus' own focus on the teaching ministry. In the tradition of the Radical Reformation and the Anabaptist movement, to which both the author of this chapter and the congregation referred to belong, the Sermon has been consistently considered the heart of Jesus' message regarding life in the light of the ethics and politics of God.

2. Permission to include the following account of Reba Place Church's unfolding story of transformation and reconciliation is acknowledged with appreciation to Mary Pat Martin and Anne Stewart who shared the initial summary. The Mennonite Church and the Church of the Brethren, together with the Society of Friends (Quakers), are usually identified as the *historic peace churches.* Their understanding of the gospel of Jesus Christ includes peace (in the biblical senses of *shalom* and *eirene*) as an essential dimension.

3. Jody Miller Shearer, *Enter the River: Healing Steps from White Privilege Toward Racial Reconciliation* (Scottdale, Penn.: Herald Press, 1994).

4. In choosing this term, *sponsoring,* we assume that there is a fundamental continuity with the ancient church practice of sponsorship. The idea is that sponsors are people who have more experience in the life and faith journey, and also possess needed resources to share with fellow travelers. The faith community is called to become a unique context of sponsorship, that is, a place conducive to growth and wholeness according to the biblical vision of a new creation and humanity.

5. Human emergence is not merely equated with psychological and sociopolitical notions of development. A key epistemological and methodological principle pertains here. The church's educational ministry must be oriented by the so-called "Chalcedonian pattern" with its three formal features: (1) *differentiation*— human and social science and biblical and theological disciplines are not confused; (2) *unity*—those and other contributions are considered side by side because they represent necessary and potentially complementary readings and visions of the human situation and hope; (3) *order*—biblical and theological views have conceptual priority. The "Chalcedonian pattern" was originally devised in the fifth century to guide the church in its understanding of Jesus Christ as both divine and human. As a *formal conceptual device,* the "Chalcedonian pattern" has been especially identified in the theology of Karl Barth.

6. Daniel S. Schipani, *Religious Education Encounters Liberation Theology* (Birmingham, Ala.: Religious Education Press, 1988); and "Liberation Theology and Christian Religious Education," in Randolph C. Miller, ed. *Theologies of Religious Education* (Birmingham, Ala.: Religious Education Press, 1995), 286-313.

7. John A. Coleman, "The Two Pedagogies: Discipleship and Citizenship," in *Education for Citizenship and Discipleship,* Mary C. Boys, ed. (New York: Pilgrim Press, 1989), chap. 2.

8. Thomas H. Groome, *Sharing Faith: A Comprehensive Approach to Religious Education and Pastoral Ministry* (San Francisco: HarperSanFrancisco, 1991), 429-31.

9. Stanley Hauerwas, *A Community of Character: Toward a Constructive Christian Social Ethic* (Notre Dame, Ind.: University of Notre Dame Press, 1981).

10. James W. Fowler, *Becoming Adult, Becoming Christian: Adult Development and Christian Faith* (San Francisco: Harper & Row, 1984), chaps. 4–5; and *Weaving the New Creation: Stages of Faith and the Public Church* (San Francisco: HarperSanFrancisco, 1991), 118-26; 157-59.

11. Sallie McFague, *Metaphorical Theology: Models of God in Religious Language* (Philadelphia: Fortress Press, 1982).

12. Coleman, 58-61.

13. For another way of describing this process of social analysis and faith reflection for action, see the four-step approach provided by Joe Holland and Peter Henroit, *Social Analysis: Linking Faith and Justice* (Maryknoll, N.Y.: Orbis Books, 1983). Four interconnected movements are identified: (1) insertion, that is, the lived commitment and engagement within contexts of poverty, injustice, and oppression; (2) social analysis, putting that experience with human suffering into a wider framework of understanding (especially by identifying factors and causes in a given situation calling for change); (3) a practical-theological reflection focusing on the questions of significance and implications regarding the participants' faith and practice; and (4) planning and action oriented toward long-term change.

14. Liberation theologians have criticized prevailing theological views of truth for failing to resonate with biblical notions of knowing and truth. Truth is related to actual historical practice, or knowing and faithfulness. Orthopraxis, rather than orthodoxy, becomes the truth criterion for theology—that is, obeying the gospel. They assert an epistemology of obedience—Christian faith must be committed participation in God's liberating and re-creating work for the sake of the world.

15. Paulo Freire, *Education for Critical Consciousness* (New York: Seabury Press, 1973); Myra Bergman Ramos, trans., *Pedagogy of the Oppressed*, rev. ed. (New York: Continuum, 1994); and Donaldo Macedo, trans. *The Politics of Education* (South Hadley, Mass.: Bergin and Garvey, 1985).

16. For further discussion of conscientization in terms of Christian education, see Mary Elizabeth Mullino Moore, *Teaching from the Heart: Theology and Educational Method* (Minneapolis: Fortress Press, 1991), chap. 6; Daniel S. Schipani, *Conscientization and Creativity: Paulo Freire and Christian Education* (Lanham, Md.: University Press of America, 1984); and R. E. Y. Wickett, *Models of Adult Religious Education* (Birmingham, Ala.: Religious Education Press, 1991), chap. 17.

17. Maria Harris, *Fashion Me a People: Curriculum in the Church* (Louisville: Westminster/John Knox Press, 1989), chap. 8.

18. James McGinnis, *Toward Compassionate and Courageous Action: A Methodology for Educating for Peace and Justice* (St. Louis: Institute for Peace and Justice, 1987); Kathleen and James McGinnis, *Parenting for Peace and Justice* (Maryknoll, N.Y.: Orbis Books, 1990).

19. R. S. Sugirtharajah, *Voices from the Margin: Interpreting the Bible in the Third World* (Maryknoll, N.Y.: Orbis Books, 1991); and Robert McAfee Brown, *Unexpected News: Reading the Bible with Third World Eyes* (Philadelphia: Westminster Press, 1984).

20. The relationship and tension between the church's mission and its educational ministry are well illustrated in Nelle G. Slater, ed., *Tensions Between Citizenship and Discipleship: A Case Study* (New York: Pilgrim Press, 1989).

21. Suzanne C. Toton, "Moving Beyond Anguish to Action: What Has Saul Alinsky to Say to Justice Education?" *Religious Education* (summer 1993): 478-93; "Moving Beyond Wordy Concern: Educating for Justice," *Union Theological Quarterly Review* (summer 1994): 39-59; and *Educating Toward a Politically Responsible Church* (Maryknoll, N.Y.: Orbis Books, 1996).

CHAPTER 3. THE FAITH COMMUNITY

1. Garry Wills, *Bare Ruined Choirs: Doubt, Prophecy, and Radical Religion* (New York: Doubleday, 1971), 37.

2. This chapter draws on the research conducted over a ten-year period by a team called the Reflective Practice Group consisting of two community psychologists, Paul R. Dokecki and J. R. Newbrough of Peabody College, Vanderbilt University, and a religious educator who is the author of this chapter. See "Community and Leadership in the Post-modern Church: I. Lessons from Latin America—the Basic Ecclesial Communities; II. The St. Robert Consultation Project; III. Leadership for Community. *P.A.C.E.: Professional Approaches for Christian Educators* 23 (October 1993): 29-33; (November 1993): 31-35; (December 1993): 36-40.

3. Robert Wuthnow, *Sharing the Journey: Support Groups and America's New Quest for Community* (New York: The Free Press, 1994), 6.

4. Ibid., 26.

5. Marcello de C. Azevedo, *Basic Ecclesial Communities in Brazil* (Washington, D.C.: Georgetown University Press, 1987).

6. Leonardo Boff, *Ecclesiogenesis: The Base Communities Reinvent the Church*, trans. Robert R. Barr (Maryknoll, N.Y.: Orbis Books, 1986).

7. See Ernesto Cardenal, *The Gospel in Solentiname*, 4 vols., trans. Donald D. Walsh (Maryknoll, N.Y.: Orbis Books, 1976–82) for an example of this interplay.

8. Gregory Baum and Robert Ellsberg, *The Logic of Solidarity: Commentaries on Pope John Paul II's Encyclical on Social Concern* (Maryknoll, N.Y.: Orbis Books, 1989).

9. Francois Houtart, *La Contribution de L'Universite Catholique de Louvain-la-Neuve au Development de la Sociologie de la Religion en Amerique Latine* (Louvin-la-Neuve, Belgium: Universite Catholique de Louvain, 1985); and Jon Sobrino, *The True Church and the Poor* (Maryknoll, N.Y.: Orbis Books, 1984).

10. The interrelationship of the two exemplifies person-in-community. J. R. Newbrough, "Community Psychology in the Post-modern World," *Journal of Community Psychology* 20 (1992): 10-25.

11. "Nothing less than a comprehensive vision of the universe is required. A new social theory, a new psychological theory, a new economic program will make no impact on the scientific-technological trance that is behind our impasse," says Brian Swimme, in Ann Lonergan and C. Richards, eds., *Thomas Berry and the New Cosmology* (Mystic, Conn.: Twenty-Third Publications, 1987).

12. The dynamics of the universe itself are *the primary revelation* of ultimate mystery. These dynamics are (1) differentiation; (2) autopoiesis (literally, saying its own name); and (3) communion. Brian Swimme and Thomas Berry, *The Uni-*

verse Story: From the Promordial Flaring Forth to the Ecozoic Era—A Celebration of the Unfolding of the Cosmos (San Francisco: HarperSanFrancisco, 1994).

13. In the congregation, community-genesis includes:

SERVICE	the primary service of the congregation is to generate and develop community life (*differentiation*)	HANDS
REFLECTION	interpretation and articulation of the word of God for the present (*autopoiesis*)	HEAD
COMMUNION	creation and maintenance of the bond within a particular church community and among such communities (*communion*)	HEART

14. Teilhard de Chardin, French Jesuit scientist and philosopher, construes the whole cosmos as the sacrament of God's loving immanence. The action of the Christ upon history in the original and new creation makes the whole universe the sacrament of God.

15. Thomas Berry, *The Dream of the Earth* (San Francisco: Sierra Club, 1988).

16. Paul R. Dokecki, "The Place of Values in the World of Psychology and Public Policy," *Peabody Journal of Education* 60 (1983): 108-25.

17. See Azevedo, *Basic Ecclesial Communities in Brazil*.

18. The work of the clergy and other pastoral agents was crucial in triggering the process of the BECs. It gave them a body of ideas, a minimum of initial organization, and a guarantee of continuity, growth, and animation. But none of that would have been successful if the idea-content had not dovetailed with the necessities of the people, or if the response had not suited their increasingly deteriorating situation in Brazil just before and after the revolution of 1964. See Azevedo, 35-36.

19. Hugh Canavan, a Carmelite missionary in Colombia who has served as a consultant to St. Robert Parish, speaks of three theological traditions for leadership. He images them as three branches of a tree: Priestly, Prophetic, Wisdom. The trunk experience is the faith community; the root experience is love (conversion). The Priestly branch is concerned with passing on the memory, the celebration of primordial events (power). The Prophetic branch announces the frustration with the present and points where to go. The Wisdom branch holds discourse on interpersonal relations, work, male/female connections, childbearing, suffering, death, and the life cycle, all oriented to the here and now—concrete situations. No one of these can be absolutized. Transformation happens with the pastor's transformation of the priesthood, turning power over to the people of the community.

20. Paul Tillich, *The Courage to Be* (New Haven, Conn.: Yale University Press, 1952).

21. Donald A. Schön, *The Reflective Practitioner: How Professionals Think in Action* (New York: Basic Books, 1983).

22. Paulo Freire, *Pedagogy of the Oppressed,* trans. Myra Bergman Ramos (New York: Herder and Herder, 1970).

23. Wendell Berry, "Health Is Membership: The Community Is the Smallest Unit of Health," *Utne Reader* (September–October 1995): 60.

CHAPTER 4. EDUCATING PERSONS

1. Rosemary Radford Ruether, *Women-Church: Theology and Practice of Feminist Liturgical Communities* (San Francisco: Harper & Row, 1985), 233-34.

2. From the editor's foreword of Bonhoeffer's *Letters and Papers from Prison,* ed. Eberhard Bethge, and trans. Reginald H. Fuller (New York: Macmillan, 1953), 9-10.

3. "The Christian moral life is finally not one of 'development' but of conversion." Stanley Hauerwas, *A Community of Character: Toward a Constructive Christian Social Ethic* (Notre Dame, Ind.: University of Notre Dame Press, 1981), 130.

4. Horace Bushnell, *Christian Nurture* (Grand Rapids, Mich.: Eerdmans, 1983), 247, 329; George Albert Coe, *The Religion of a Mature Mind* (Chicago: Fleming H. Revell, 1902), 306.

5. Martin Buber, *I and Thou,* trans. S. G. Smith (1958; reprint, New York: Simon & Schuster, 1978). Buber's philosophy is a reminder that any Christian retrieval of person has to be aware of the Jewish context of Christological reflection. Although the debates that issued in the category of person took place in Greek, Christians were actually struggling with Jewish history more than Greek philosophy. The Jews did not have the inclination or the occasion to work out such a philosophical concept. But Jewish (and later Muslim) thinkers shared some history with the Christians, and if only rarely, some conversation. Today the single best defense against a rerun of conservative Christian versus liberal religious education is a dialogue with Jewish thought. A Christian form of religious education can only be worked out in relation to a Jewish form of religious education.

6. Paulo Freire, *Pedagogy of the Oppressed* (New York: Herder and Herder, 1970). See also his *Education for Critical Consciousness* (New York: Seabury Press, 1973).

7. See, for example, *Illuminations of Hildegard of Bingen* (Santa Fe, N.M.: Bear & Co., 1985; Simone Weil, *Waiting for God* (New York: Harper & Row, 1951); Thich Nhat Hanh *Peace Is Every Step,* ed. Arthur Kotler (New York: Bantam, 1991); Anthony de Mello, *Sadhana: A Way to God* (Garden City, N.Y.: Doubleday, 1984).

8. On *lectio divina,* see Macrina Wiederkehr, *The Song of the Seed: The Monastic Way of Tending the Soul* (San Francisco: HarperSanFrancisco, 1995); on modern saints, see Bonhoeffer, *Letters and Papers from Prison*; Helen Prejean, *Dead Man Walking: An Eyewitness Account of the Death Penalty in the United States* (New York: Random House, 1993); and Etty Hillesum, *An Interrupted Life: The Diaries of Etty Hillesum 1941–1943* (New York: Pantheon Books, 1983). See chapter 5, "Nourishing," in Maria Harris, *Dance of the Spirit* (New York: Bantam, 1989), 114-44.

9. See Thomas Keating, Basil Pennington, and Thomas Clarke, *Finding Grace at the Center* (Petersham, Mass.: St. Bede's Publications, 1985).

10. See Theodore Roethke, "The Abyss" from *Collected Poems* (London: Chatto and Windus Ltd., 1963).

11. From Walter Brueggemann's commentary on the book of Exodus in *The New Interpreter's Bible* (Nashville: Abingdon Press, 1994), 845.

12. G. K. Chesterton, *Orthodoxy* (Garden City, N.Y.: Doubleday, 1959), 48.

13. Jean Piaget and Barbel Inhelder, *The Psychology of the Child* (New York: Basic Books, 1969).

14. Erik Erikson, *The Child and Society,* 2nd ed. (New York: Norton, 1963).

15. Lyn Mikel Brown and Carol Gilligan, *Meeting at the Crossroads: Women's Psychology and Girls' Development* (Cambridge, Mass.: Harvard University Press, 1992).

16. See Gabriel Moran, *Religious Education Development* (Minneapolis: Winston Press, 1983), chap. 6; Maria Harris, "Completion and Faith Development," in *Faith Development and Fowler,* ed. Craig Dykstra and Sharon Parks (Birmingham, Ala.: Religious Education Press, 1986), 115-33.

17. James Fowler, *Faith Development* (San Francisco: Harper & Row, 1981); *Becoming Adult, Becoming Christian* (San Francisco: Harper & Row, 1984).

18. An Eastern view would be a helpful comparison on this point; for example, the *Tao Te Ching*: "He who pursues Tao will decrease every day." Among psychologists, James Hillman has been the most helpfully critical of growth; see Hillman's *The Dream and the Underworld* (New York: HarperCollins, 1979).

19. John Demos, *A Little Commonwealth* (New York: Oxford University Press, 1970), 146.

20. For the meaning of conversion in Christian life, see Joanmarie Smith, *A Context for Christianity in the Twenty-First Century* (Allen, Tex.: Thomas More, 1995).

21. For examples, see John Dominic Crossan, *Jesus: A Biographical Portrait* (San Francisco: HarperSanFrancisco, 1994); Gerd Theissen, *The Sociology of Early Palestinian Christianity* (Philadelphia: Fortress Press, 1978); and Wayne A. Meeks, *The Origins of Christian Morality: The First Two Centuries* (New Haven, Conn.: Yale University Press, 1993).

22. Thomas Moore, *Care of the Soul* (New York: HarperCollins, 1992).

23. Eugene Boyer, *High School: A Report on Secondary Education in America* (New York: Harper & Row, 1983), 202-15.

24. The standard cliché in ecological writing is that "the Judeo-Christian tradition" is the cause of our ecological problems because "man" was placed at the top of creation and everything else was reduced to a utilitarian purpose. The reference to Judeo-Christian tradition guarantees there will be no examination of the actual histories of Judaism and Christianity. The assumption that "man" was the end of all things neglects the most fundamental relation of the divine and the human. In both Jewish and Christian imagery the humans are the center, not the top; they represent all creation. In short, Christianity is confused with Comtean positivism of the nineteenth century; Auguste Comte had no doubt that putting "man" at the top required getting rid of Christianity.

CHAPTER 5. RELIGIOUS INSTRUCTION: HOMEMAKING

1. The vision for this kind of class belonged to Noel Beck who was a member and officer of this congregation. Her dream about a class that could transform teaching and learning and her commitment to making it happen enabled this experience of homemaking to take place.

2. Mary Catherine Bateson, *Peripheral Visions: Learning Along the Way* (New York: HarperCollins, 1995), 213.

3. Sharon Daloz Parks, "Home and Pilgrimage: Companion Metaphors for Personal and Social Transformation," *Soundings* 72 (summer/fall 1989): 304.

4. Sara Little, *To Set One's Heart: Belief and Teaching in the Church* (Atlanta: John Knox Press, 1983), 5.

5. Letty Russell, *Household of Freedom: Authority in Feminist Theology* (Philadelphia: Westminster Press, 1987), 87.

6. Nelle Morton, *The Journey Is Home* (Boston: Beacon Press, 1985), xix.

7. Thanks to Maria Harris who has presented the concept of various forms of curriculum contributing to an integrated approach to congregational ministry in her book, *Fashion Me a People: Curriculum in the Church* (Louisville: Westminster/ John Knox Press, 1989).

8. Parks, 304.

9. This is a concept used by Carol Lakey Hess in her forthcoming work, *Caretakers of Our Common House: Women's Development in Communities of Faith* (Nashville: Abingdon Press).

10. Ibid.

11. Parks, 304.

12. My thanks to my colleague and dean, Heidi Hadsell, for sharing this story with me.

13. Parker Palmer, *To Know as We Are Known: A Spirituality of Education* (San Francisco: HarperSanFrancisco, 1993), 69.

14. Thanks to Beverly Cheney and her wise insights about people and process in learning communities, which she used so effectively in her teaching at the First Presbyterian Church in Florence, Alabama.

15. Harris, 48.

16. bell hooks, *Teaching to Transgress: Education as the Practice of Freedom* (New York: Routledge, 1994), 39.

17. C. Roland Christensen, "Premises and Practices of Discussion Teaching," in *Education for Judgment: The Artistry of Discussion Leadership,* ed. C. Roland Christensen, David A. Garvin, and Ann Sweet (Boston: Harvard Business School Press, 1991), 19.

18. These concepts of knowing, interpreting, living, and doing when combined with "the Word," were originally used as names of four curricula produced by an ecumenical partnership of denominations in the 1970s under the name of "Joint Educational Development." I believe they capture the nature and task of religious education with all persons of faith.

19. See Hess, *Caretakers of Our Common House.*

20. Jack L. Seymour, Margaret Ann Crain, and Joseph V. Crockett, *Educating Christians: The Intersection of Meaning, Learning, and Vocation* (Nashville: Abingdon Press, 1993), 185.

21. Russell, *Household of Freedom,* 91.

22. Ibid., 37.

CHAPTER 7. LISTENING TO CHURCHES: CHRISTIAN EDUCATION IN CONGREGATIONAL LIFE

1. See Letty Russell, *Growth in Partnership* (Philadelphia: Westminster Press, 1981), 105, 154.

2. For a fuller discussion of ethnography, see Margaret Ann Crain and Jack L.

Seymour, "The Ethnographer as Minister: Ethnographic Research in Ministry," in *Religious Education* 91 (summer 1996), 299-315.

3. For a fuller discussion of just and hospitable space, see Jack L. Seymour, Margaret Ann Crain, and Joseph V. Crockett, *Educating Christians: The Intersection of Meaning, Learning, and Vocation* (Nashville: Abingdon Press, 1993), 90-91.

4. Charles R. Foster, *Educating Congregations: The Future of Christian Education* (Nashville: Abingdon Press, 1994), 45.

5. Margaret Ann Crain and Jack L. Seymour, "The Cry for Theology II: Laity Speak About the Church," *P.A.C.E.: Professional Approaches for Christian Educators* 25 (March 1996), 43-46.

6. Seymour, Crain, and Crockett, 89-95.

7. For a fuller discussion of this, see Parker Palmer, *To Know as We Are Known: A Spirituality of Education* (San Francisco: Harper & Row), 1983.

8. Seymour, Crain, and Crockett, 145.

9. Brother Lawrence of the Resurrection, *The Practice of the Presence of God*, trans. and introduction, John J. Delaney (New York: Doubleday Image Book, 1977), 68.

10. See chapter 1, p. 17.

CHAPTER 8: AGENDA FOR THE FUTURE

1. *Reflections on Brethren Image and Identity* (Elgin, Ill.: Brethren Press, 1995), 59.

2. Mary C. Boys, *Educating in Faith: Maps and Visions* (St. Louis: Sheed and Ward, 1993).

3. See Margaret Ann Crain and Jack Seymour, "The Cry for Theology I: Laity Speak About Theology," *P.A.C.E.: Professional Approaches for Christian Educators* (February 1996), 29-34; "The Cry for Theology II: Laity Speak About the Church," *P.A.C.E.* (March 1996), 43-46; "Thrashing in the Night: Laity Speak About Religious Knowing," *Religious Education* (spring 1997).

4. Robert Bellah et al., *Habits of the Heart: Individualism and Commitment in American Life* (Berkeley: University of California Press, 1985).

5. Craig Dykstra, "Between the Times: Changing Denominations in a Changing Culture" (presentation for the meeting of U.S. Church Leaders, Dallas, Tex., February 29, 1996); and Robert J. Wuthnow, "The Shifting Focus of Faith" (paper presented at the meeting of U.S. Church Leaders, Dallas, Tex., February 29, 1996), 8-9.

6. Sara Little, "The 'Clue' to Religious Education," *Union Seminary Quarterly Review* 47 (1993): 20.

7. Ibid.

8. The Carter Center, in Atlanta, Georgia, supports peaceful social change and human development. It was founded by former president Jimmy Carter.

9. "Looking at the World Upside Down: An Interview with Robert Coles," *Christian Century* 110 (December 1, 1993): 1208.

10. Ibid., 1210-11.

11. Jack L. Seymour, Margaret Ann Crain, and Joseph V. Crockett, *Educating Christians: The Intersection of Meaning, Learning, and Vocation* (Nashville: Abingdon Press, 1994), 50-52.

12. Ibid., 151.

13. Samuel Amirtham and John S. Pobee, eds. *Theology by the People: Reflections on Doing Theology in Community* (Geneva: World Council of Churches, 1986), ix.

14. Diana L. Eck, *Encountering God: A Spiritual Journey from Bozeman to Banaras* (Boston: Beacon Press, 1993), 2.
15. Ibid.
16. Ibid., 15.
17. Crain and Seymour, "The Cry for Theology II," 43.
18. Crain and Seymour, "Thrashing in the Night," 1.
19. Crain and Seymour, "The Cry for Theology II," 44.

CONTRIBUTORS

Elizabeth Caldwell is Professor of Educational Ministry at McCormick Theological Seminary in Chicago. She is an ordained minister in the Presbyterian Church (U.S.A.).

Margaret Ann Crain, a United Methodist, is Diaconal Minister of Christian Education at Peachtree Road United Methodist Church in Atlanta, Georgia.

Maria Harris, a Roman Catholic, has held the Howard Chair in Religious Education at Andover Newton Theological School and the Tuohy Chair in Interrreligious Studies at John Carroll University.

Donald E. Miller is General Secretary for the Church of the Brethren in Elgin, Illinois. A Brethren minister, he was previously Alvin F. Brightbill Professor of Ministry Studies at Bethany Theological Seminary.

Gabriel Moran is Professor of Religious Education in the Department of Culture and Communication at New York University. He is a Roman Catholic.

Robert T. O'Gorman, a Roman Catholic, is Associate Professor of Pastoral Studies and Director of Field Education at Loyola University of Chicago.

Daniel S. Schipani, an ordained minister in the Mennonite Church, is Professor of Christian Education and Personality at Associated Mennonite Biblical Seminary in Elkhart, Indiana.

Jack L. Seymour, an ordained United Methodist minister, is Academic Dean and Professor of Religious Education at Garrett-Evangelical Theological Seminary in Evanston, Illinois.